Latinas in VC

A MASTER GUIDE TO THE VOICES, STRATEGIES, AND STORIES OF LATINAS AND WOMEN IN VENTURE CAPITAL

LAURA MORENO LUCAS

For more information contact:
www.figfactormedia.com

Cover Design and Layout by DG Marco Antonio Álvarez Rodríguez
Printed in the United States of America

ISBN: 978-1-961600-49-2

Library of Congress Control Number: 2025902145

Latinas
in VC

Service
www.hopenn.com

DEDICATION

This book is dedicated to the investor community that is making a difference—tipping the scales of capital toward women and empowering them to build billion-dollar businesses.

aurora
PRIX-FIXE
BRUNCH
Saturday & Sunday
11:00 am to 3:45 pm
COCKTAILS
HAPPY HOUR

ACKNOWLEDGMENTS

I am deeply grateful to all the authors, sponsors, and our publisher, Fig Factor Media Publishing. Your support and generosity have made this book possible at a time when uplifting all voices is more important than ever. This book is dedicated to those whose voices have gone unheard or have been left behind—to remind you that you are seen, you are valued, and you belong. In a world where many of us have had to fight relentlessly to make this happen, know that your presence and story matter.

As I look toward the next generation, my heart is full of hope. There is an incredible opportunity ahead, and many of the inspiring individuals in this book have paved the way for you to rise.

I would like to acknowledge all the Libra Leaders who have created this incredible network of women dedicated to supporting one another. I especially want to recognize Cecilia Sanchez and Stephanie Michael Silva for their tireless efforts in building a powerful ecosystem of capital for women.

Finally, to the most incredible person in my life—my mother, Aurora. She is a gentle and quiet woman, but her discipline and unwavering care have given me the spirit to lead with empathy and see the world through a lens of kindness. Thank you, Mama. I love you!

1.98%
Net Change
+347.87
17,889.41
Net Change
+0.83
amazon
0.62%
Net Change
+1.15
Stock Price
$185.8
STARBUCKS
2.43%
Net Change
-1.82
Stock Price
$73.11
SBUX
6.76%
Net Change
+11.70
Stock Price
$184.73
AAPL
PEP
L'ATTITUDE
VENTURES
Nasdaq
NOPALERA

INTRODUCTION

With great pride, I introduce *Latinas in VC!* This book highlights some of the most courageous, forward-thinking women in finance and brings together visionary venture capitalists into one convenient resource.

The women profiled in this book empathize with the Latina and women investor experience. They have fearlessly built and launched their own investment platforms in a world where less than 2% of capital is deployed to women. The Latinas in this book are highly successful, driven, and structured to invest in high-growth opportunities. They share my mission for making a difference among founders with a dream.

Some of the Latinas in this book are like me: immigrants to the country who arrived and found their way into the world of venture capital. I was seven years old when I came to this country from Guadalajara without knowing the language. My struggle with the language barrier taught me resilience and perseverance, which became my superpower to achieve life's goals.

One of my first goals was to complete my education and earn a degree in criminal justice. I wanted to become an FBI agent, but they told me to get more life experience before applying. So, I found an entry-level job at a finance firm. There, I was introduced to investing. I watched incredulously as millions of dollars flowed through Wall Street to build wealth for others in our capital markets. I was fascinated with the availability of funds and the idea of helping create and grow something.

In the late 2000s, I became NASDAQ's Managing Director of New Listings and Capital Markets. It was an exciting time for tech, and I saw today's billionaires in the making. I helped close the IPOs of giants like Lyft, Beyond Meat, Airbnb, and RealReal. When the CEO of RealReal asked me how many other women-owned companies had IPO'd, I could only find 20 in NASDAQ's then 30-year history.

In 2022, I joined L'ATTITUDE Ventures and we announced our $100M institutional venture capital platform for early-stage innovative companies led by U.S. Latinos. I am proud to say we have since made 32 investments with an average check size of $1.6M in capital to each startup! I am also a part of Libra Leaders, where we tip the scales of capital to early stage women entrepreneurs.

Through my work in venture capital and *Latinas in VC*, my mission is to continue highlighting the need in the capital markets and place resources and opportunities into the hands of aspiring entrepreneurs. Working together, we can empower each other, successfully fund businesses, and bring unique products to market that appeal to a broader demographic. We can create vast venture capital ecosystems offering the opportunity and vision currently lacking for founders.

I hope this book inspires you to take the next step toward your dream. And perhaps, within the network of incredibly talented women in this book, you may find the perfect venture capital partner to make it come true. If so, I will consider it a mission accomplished. Here's wishing you great success in your venture!

Laura Moreno Lucas
L'ATTITUDE Ventures

PREFACE

I first met Laura at my graduation ceremony when I earned my master's degree in marketing from the University of Denver. She was dating my son, Brian, and they had both flown in for the ceremony from San Francisco. We hit it off immediately - fortunate, since she became my daughter-in-law soon after.

Laura and I come from vastly different professions, yet our communication skills are critical to our livelihoods. Laura needs to be an expert communicator to vet the budding entrepreneurs she intends to support and to understand their ability to lead a business successfully.

For me, after working for many decades in television journalism and higher education, I now serve on the executive committee of the board of directors for the National Academy of Television Arts and Sciences (NATAS), which governs the Daytime, News and Documentary, Sports, Tech, and Children's & Family Emmy Awards. I received the Heartland Board of Governors Award - an Emmy - in 2024 for my service to this regional chapter. And, with my background in communications and journalism, I was thrilled when I heard Laura was spearheading this book project.

While everyone has grappled with professional issues, Laura has faced extraordinary challenges in becoming the success she is today.

She graduated from college, eventually making her way into a high profile position in the highly competitive venture capital world where few other Latina women have dared to tread.

I see so many admirable qualities in Laura that create the fearless powerhouse she is today. Laura has a unique ability to reach people on emotional and technical levels. She intuits the heart and soul of an entrepreneur pitching their ideas but accurately assesses the conceptual ultimate return on investment. Her can-do spirit and collaborative nature make her an excellent mentor and partner with a genuine optimism that inspires everyone around her.

While Laura has soft skills to connect with others, her aspirations remain. She is undeterred by traditional obstacles, earning respect in everything she does. Being one of few women in a male-dominated field, she must advocate for herself and navigate the choppy waters of an industry where men historically take the lead.

She succeeds because she regards her Latino heritage as a strength that helps her achieve her goals with patience and hard work. She embraces her identity and continues moving forward toward the ambitious objectives she continually sets for herself.

Outside the boardroom, Laura impresses me with her multitasking as a wife, mother, and half of a true power couple. Laura and Brian gave me the greatest gift possible when my granddaughter Adriana was born. She is the image of her mother - fearless, confident, happy and grounded - and is a walking illustration of “girl power” and prepared to do amazing things. Despite their busy schedules, Laura and Brian share child and household duties 50/50 while supporting each other in their individual and collective ventures. I’m proud of what they have achieved together and individually, and most of all, for the example they set for Adriana.

Laura’s Latina background and work ethic have enhanced our family, whose ancestors were Irish, Scottish, German and Swedish immigrants. I hope *Latinas in VC* reaches a broad leadership, opening the eyes of people from different backgrounds who may not look beyond the standard solution.

In the right hands, this book can help investors understand how those from different cultures can provide far richer ideas and creative solutions to problems. While we know people's backgrounds are relevant to how and why they succeed, Laura's success is largely due to vision, aspiration, patience, and hard work - all qualities needed for entrepreneurs to succeed in venture capital.

Latinas in VC offers many examples of people poised to help others achieve the success they deserve. Thank you, Laura, for this gift to the venture capital world.

Julie Lucas
Executive Committee
National Academy of Television Arts and Sciences

TABLE OF CONTENTS

 COMPANY NAME

 LOCATION

 AUM/INVESTMENT TOTAL

 BIOGRAPHY

 THESIS/STRATEGY

 PORTFOLIO COMPANIES/ INVESTMENTS

 FOUNDER ADVICE

 FUNDER ADVICE

Monica
Brand Engel

Co-Founder and Managing Partner

QUONA

Washington, DC, and global

$800 million AUM

Monica Brand Engel, Co-Founder and Managing Partner of Quona Capital, is an investor and entrepreneur, who has spent her career dedicated to broadening financial inclusion globally. She spent her formative years in Silicon Valley, building alternative financing companies targeted at near-bankable businesses. With a desire to apply lessons learned in emerging markets, she moved to South Africa after graduating Stanford Business School to work in venture capital in a nascent ecosystem. From Cape Town, Monica was recruited by Accion as Head of Product and Innovation to launch new financial services for underserved businesses and consumers globally. Her experience includes a period in Mexico with Compartamos Bank, Latin America's largest microfinance institute and re-branded Gentera Bank following its initial public offering (IPO) in 2007. This IPO provided the funds to launch Accion's Frontier Investments – its first fintech for inclusion fund and the predecessor to the creation of Quona Capital – venture and growth equity firm focused on inclusive fintech in emerging markets. Monica leads the Africa, Middle East and North Africa (MENA), and cross-border investment strategy at Quona. She's half Peruvian and blessed with a fantastic husband and twins.

Inclusive fintech in emerging markets.

Compartamos (IPO), Shubham (acquired by Premji Invest), Zoona (acquired by Chipper Cash), Tiaxa (acquired by BeMobi), Azimo (acquired by Papaya), Yoco, Verto, Twinco, Khazna, Octa, and Maxsoko

Fight for things you care about, but do it in a way that will lead others to join you.

Fulfillment is like finance: the greatest of life's rewards accrue to those willing to take the risk.

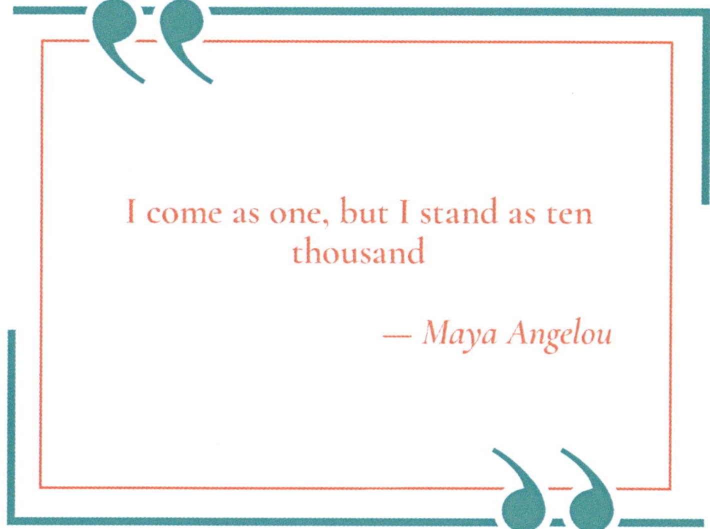
I come as one, but I stand as ten thousand

— *Maya Angelou*

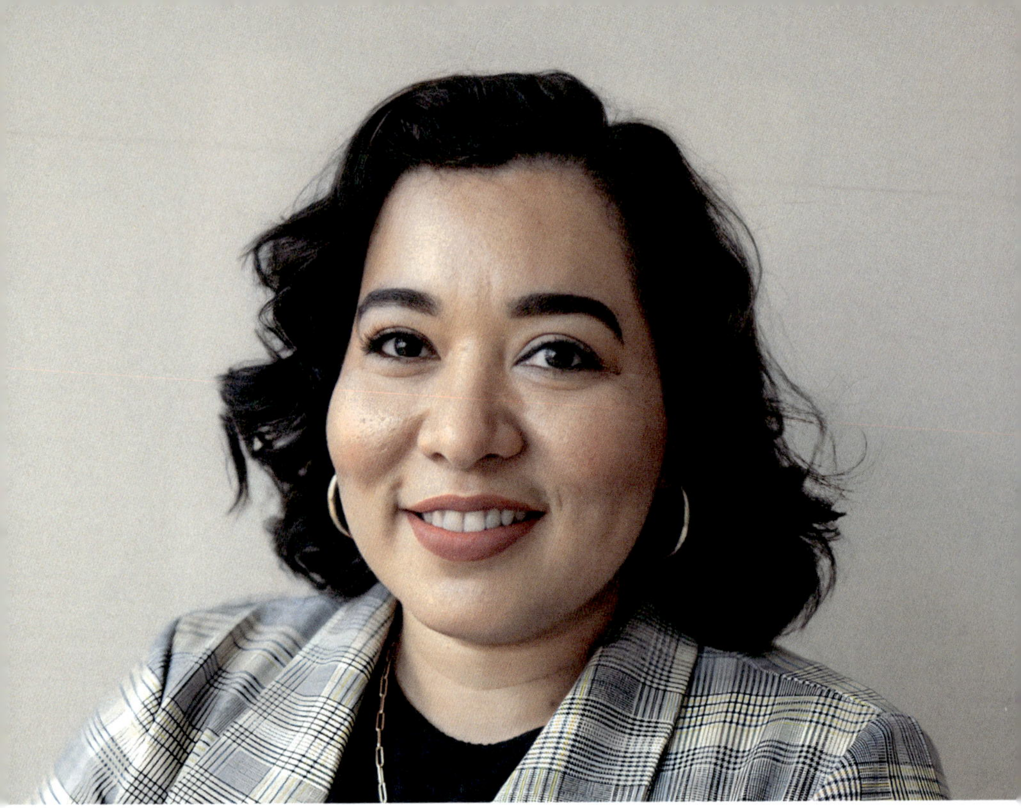

Noramay
Cadena

Managing Partner

Los Angeles, California

$50 million AUM

Noramay Cadena is the Managing Partner of Supply Change Capital, a venture capital firm investing in technology to transform the food system. Over the last ten years, Noramay has invested in over ninety companies across industries and stages. Prior to her career as an investor, Noramay spent over a decade in the aerospace industry as an engineer and operations leader. In 2024, she was recognized as an Inspiring Emerging Manager by Annenberg Foundation's PledgeLA and as a Pioneer Woman of the Year by the Los Angeles Commission on the Status of Women. In 2022, she was recognized as one of ten women of influence in private markets by PEI . She's also been named one of fifty-five risingstar VCs who shook up the industry (2021), one of fifty renowned women in robotics (2020), and was named one of the top 100 influential Latinas in the United States by Latino Leaders Magazine from 2020-2022. She's an original cofounder of Latinas in STEM (2013) and SomosVC (2019), a Kauffman Fellow, and holds three degrees from the Massachusetts Institute of Technology. She was born in Mexico and lives in Los Angeles with her husband and young son, not far from her daughter.

Investing in technology to transform the food system.

We have invested in 24 companies

Entrepreneurship success requires so much personally and professionally. Be a good human, envision the long term, but act locally, quickly, and methodically. Learn fast and communicate with clarity and transparency.

As my mom often reminded me growing up with the saying, "Dime con quién andas y te diré quien eres," company is everything. In venture, we're building mini-ecosystems and who you can inspire to lean in to support, make introductions, or co-invest is unique to you, essential, and can mean the difference between portfolio success or failure.

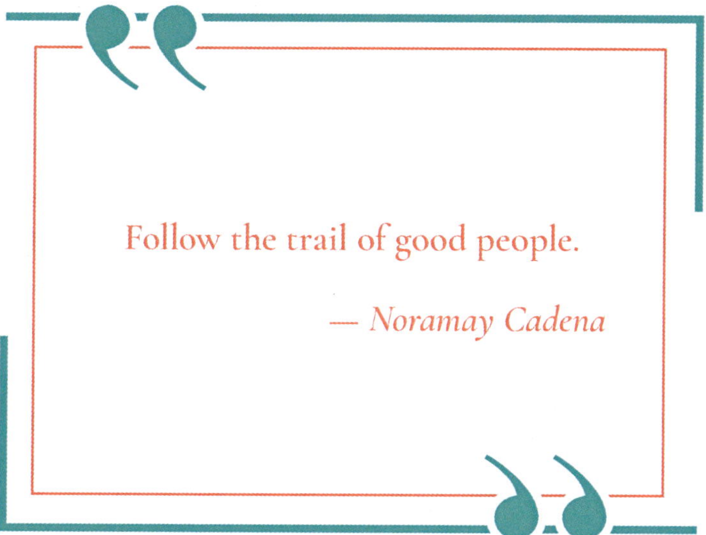

Follow the trail of good people.

— Noramay Cadena

Kimberli Cavazos Haywood

Director of Investments

CANDIDE GROUP

Utah and California

$175 million/$240 million invested AUM

Kimberli Cavazos Haywood is a Chicana activist, investor and seasoned community development practitioner with over two decades of experience driving deep community impact. She has led transformative community reinvestment programs for major financial institutions, helping deploy billions of dollars into some of America's most underinvested communities. As an allocator, Kim has directed nearly $400 million to more than 50 fund managers, focused on economic growth and opportunity. A passionate advocate for equity and justice, Kim has served on numerous nonprofit boards and dedicated her career to addressing systemic inequities. Her contributions have been recognized with multiple awards for outstanding achievements. Kim earned a bachelor's degree in communications from the University of Utah. A proud third-generation Mexican American, she is the devoted mother of four young men and has shared over twenty-five years of partnership with her beloved husband.

Candide Group works with impact-oriented investors who have a shared belief that finance can serve as a tool of empowerment rather than a weapon of extraction. We seek innovative structures where there are both capital needs and opportunities for mission-aligned investors to build impactful investment portfolios.

We have invested in over 140 fund managers or entrepreneurs, such as Chingona Ventures, Symphonic Capital, Kapor and Fresno Area Hispanic Foundation.

Lead with your passion, embrace your authenticity, and surround yourself with smart people.

Understand who, how, and what your money will impact in the world.

The process of empowerment cannot be simplistically defined in accordance with our own particular class interests. We must learn to lift as we climb.

— *Angela Davis*

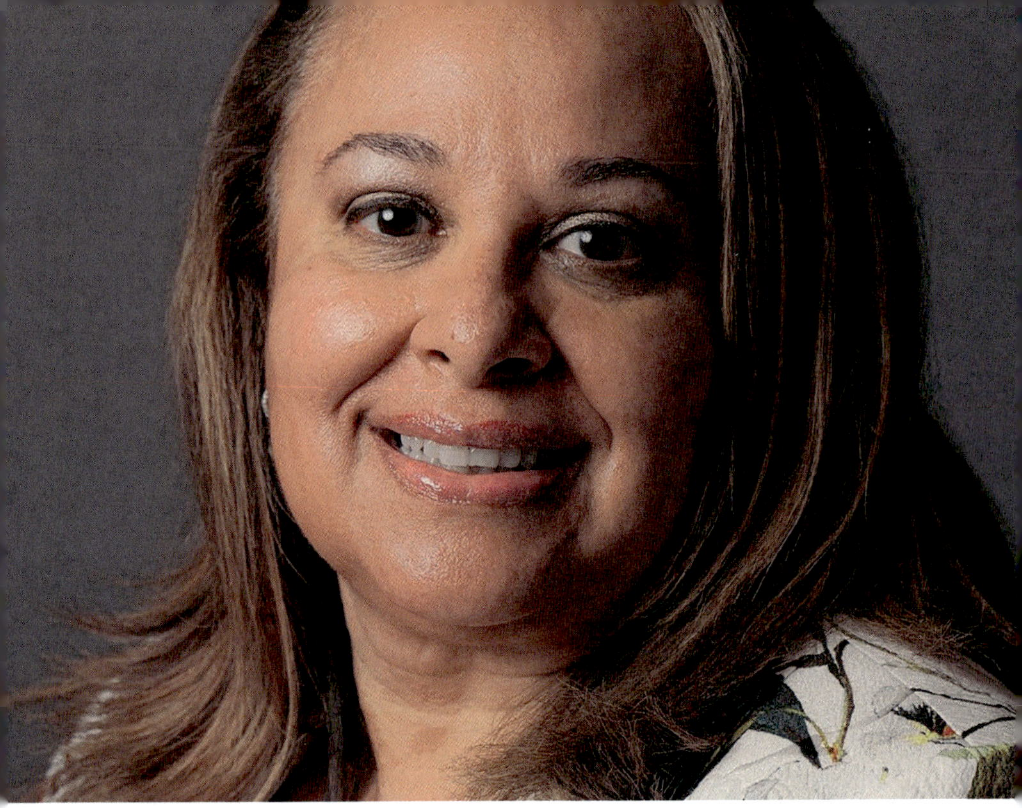

Adela
Cepeda

Chair and Co-founder

Chicago

$20 million to $30 million AUM

Adela Cepeda is an independent corporate director of BMO Financial Corp., and of the Pathway Funds, and chairs the UBS and Mercer Funds. Adela is chair of Angeles Investors, an angel investing group she co-founded in 2020, which now has approximately 500 members throughout the United States. She is co-general partner of Angeles Ventures Fund I. Adela has been recognized with the Leadership Greater Chicago Distinguished Fellow Award, the Silicon Valley Lifetime Leadership Award, and the Latina Trailblazer Award by Latino Justice. She was included among the 100 Most Influential Latinos by Bloomberg Linea and included among the 50 Most Powerful Latinas by ALPFA. She has been named to the NACD Directorship 100, a recognition given to the most influential leaders in corporate governance. Adela completed her master's degree in business administration at the University of Chicago and her bachelor of arts degree from Harvard College. She has received honorary doctorate degrees from Metropolitan College of New York and Dominican University.

Seed stage companies with disruptive potential, mostly technology

Canela Media, Certiverse, Linker Finance, and MasPanadas

- Think long-term but execute now.
- First time funds are highly rewarding, so be bold.

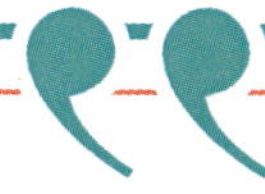

Investing with the mission to help close the Latina wealth gap fuels my drive to succeed NOW.

— *Adela Cepeda*

Marta
Cruz

Co-founder & General Partner

NXTP VENTURES

Buenos Aires, Argentina

$180 million AUM

Co-founder & General Partner

B2B tech early stage startups

225, AuthO, Nuvemshop, Frete, Spline, Arquivei, Teachi, Barte.

Invest with purpose.

Learn from mistakes.

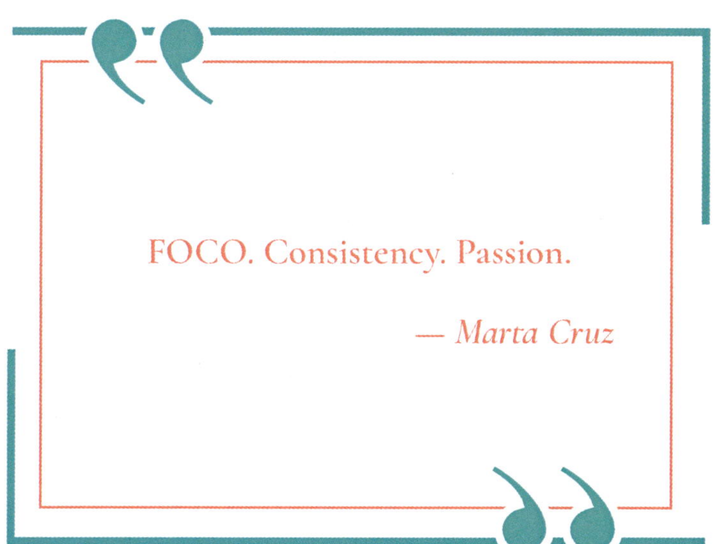

Susana
Espinosa De Los Reyes

Partner

DUX

Austin, Texas and Mexico City, Mexico

$20 million AUM

Susana is the newest addition to the DUX capital team even though her collaboration goes back to more than five years. As an investor, Susana has a diversity and inclusion focus after co-founding Mujeres Invirtiendo, an industry-focused NGO to promote and empower the role of female investors in the Private Equity industry.

Susana holds an MBA from Instituto de Empresa Madrid (IE Business School), and a Master's in International Development from ITAM in Mexico where she previously studied her Bachelor's in Administration. Prior to joining Dux Capital, Susana was Portfolio Manager for Angel Ventures, a top-tier VC fund in the region. Susana was in charge of the day to day of portfolio companies in order to help them develop and grow. Susana has expertise in managing companies from their seed stage up to their exit.

Aside from this, Susana has entrepreneurial expertise in founding Carpe Diem, a boutique mindful training fitness studio in Mexico where she currently holds a seat on their Board. Susana has been selected as a top emerging investor by LAVCA (Latin America Venture Capital Association) due to her commitment to gender diversity in the industry. Also, Susana has focused on teaching others about entrepreneurship. Currently, she has a lecture at Instituto Tecnológico Autónomo de México (ITAM).

Seed stage venture

We have invested in Koa, Innovare, Pura Mente, Cubbo, Cheddies, Mozper, Fintonic.

Never change your strategy to fit what an investor wants. Follow your path.

Your business partners and team determine your success, always surround yourself with people you admire and who help you become a better investor.

La vida no es la que uno vivió sino la que uno recuerda y como la recuerda para contarla.

— *Gabriel Garcia Marquez*

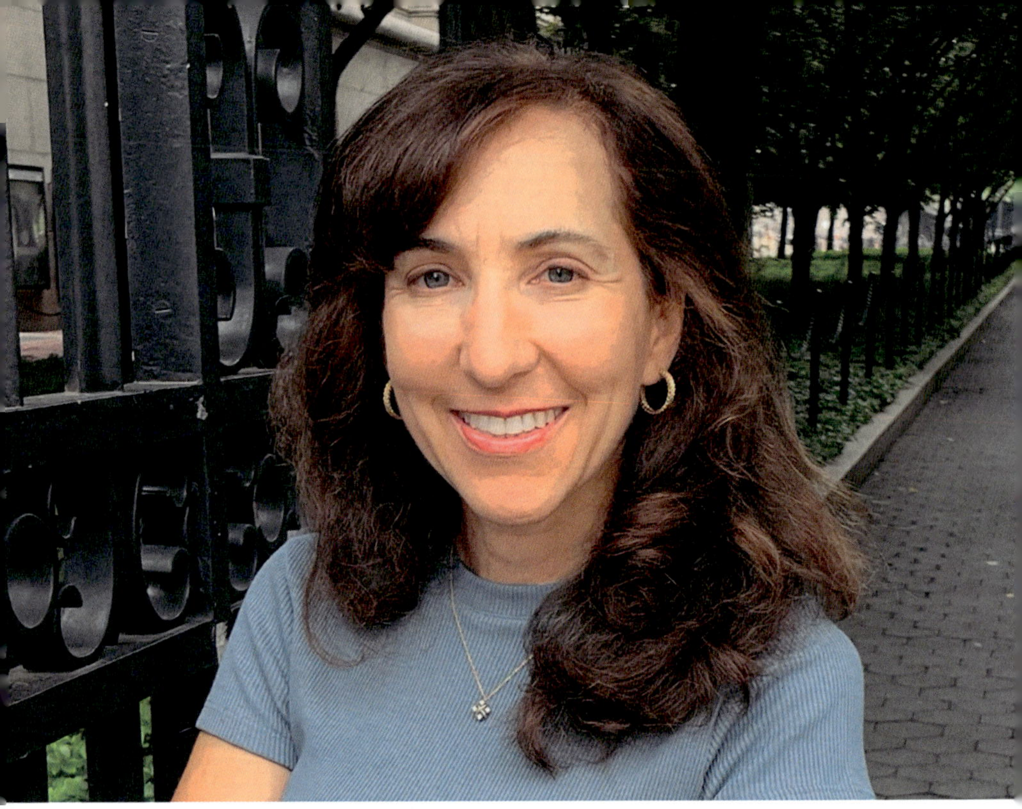

Joy Fairbanks

Managing Principal/ Operating and Investment Partner/ Partner

Los Angeles, San Francisco, and New York

Emerging Fund (Portola Valley Partners/Silicon Valley Women Founders Fund). Targeting over $25 million in the first 18 months. Rolling up to $100 million AUM

Joy Fairbanks is an experienced institutional investor, builder, innovation advisor, and educator. She works extensively with founders of early-stage tech startups across sectors and verticals.

Joy is Managing Principal at Fairbanks Venture Advisors (FVA) and an Operating and Investment Partner at Portola Valley Partners (PVP) focused on enabling innovative tech ventures with high performing and underrepresented founders. At PVP, Joy helped set in motion the launch of the Silicon Valley Women Founders Fund where she will serve as a Partner. PVP is an associate producer of the award-winning documentary, Show Her the Money, focused on the journey of women founders and capital allocators.

As Managing Principal of FVA, Joy works with emerging investors and VCs on developing investment theses, crafting robust founder and startup valuation rubrics, drafting performance tracking/reporting, sourcing investments, and cultivating individual and institutional LPs. Additionally, Joy works with universities, investors, and corporate clients on innovation programming, platforms, and advisory.

Joy's superpower is identifying high potential founders and guiding them to success. Joy advises over a hundred tech startup founders per year across sectors and geographies on product development, market assessment/customer acquisition strategy, partnerships/pilots, financial forecasting, funding, M&A, turnarounds, and exits. She is a requested speaker and university lecturer on these topics and writes about startup success at FairbanksVentureAdvisors.com.

Joy has launched and provided support to various tech incubators across the US and abroad including Techstars, Blackstone, Village Capital, Venture Out, Columbia Venture Community 2.8 Women's Accelerator, LBAN/Latino Business Action Network, Stanford's Hacking for Recovery, Cal Hacks, NYU's New Media Accelerator, and the Long Beach Accelerator. She is the founder of two management consulting practices.

Joy has served as a faculty member of entrepreneurship at Columbia Business School where she organized Columbia's first cross-campus startup hackathon and ran the impact venture incubator course. Joy has an MBA in finance from Columbia Business School, a Masters in International History from the London School of Economics and Political Science, and a Bachelors in Economics from UC Berkeley.

Tech. People. Impact. Investing in intellectual property (IP)-driven, customer-centered technology led by high energy founders with insight into (and a burning desire to solve) problems that matter. Sector agnostic but favoring investments with the biggest positive impact on people and the planet. Seeking innovative software applications and technologies at early revenue stage or in pilots close to launch. Allocating capital to women and underrepresented founders. Tech driven LatinX founders are a natural fit given grit, talent, lived experiences, community values, and high success standards.

Emerging Fund.

Always focus on being a partner with your customer to solve specific problems with broad market applications. Your own insight and data into this customer experience, and your value add, trumps any contrarian opinions. Prove a non-consensus, large-market opportunity. Build collaboratively and nurture relationships, especially with your own nascent team. Don't be afraid to pivot. It's okay to regroup. Always be learning.

Invest according to your values. If you invest to enable solutions for problems you really care about (and know something about), you will naturally find lucrative opportunities. Data and your own due diligence should not be swayed by a good storyteller and crowd excitement. If it seems too good to be true or if you don't understand it, pause. Hard stuff can be simple when viewed in individual, clearly communicated components. Trust what you bring to the table.

Enabling innovation and capturing market opportunities is about creating lasting relationships with thoughtful people with a bias towards action.

— Joy Fairbanks

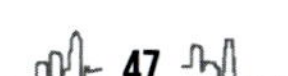

Maria
Gutierrez Peñaloza

Co-founding Partner

NIDO VENTURES

Los Angeles, California

$7 million AUM

Maria Gutierrez Peñaloza is the co-founder and managing partner at Nido Ventures, a venture capital fund that invests in pre-seed and seed B2B technology companies transforming foundational industries in the United States-Mexico corridor. As a Forbes 30 Under 30 honoree and with experience as an angel investor, her leadership has enabled Nido Ventures to secure support from notable investors, like Bill Gates' daughter, Jennifer Gates, and achieve significant portfolio growth within the first two years of operation. Originating from Mexico City, she plays a significant role in the United States and LATAM technology and the venture capital space. She has previously held key positions in logistics and semiconductor procurement at Tesla and Apple, managing over $800 million. Maria earned a bachelor of science in management science and engineering and a master in business administration, both from Stanford University.

Nido Ventures invests in pre-seed B2B technology companies transforming foundational industries in the United States-Mexico corridor.

Maqui, Palenca, Alohome, Soyplenna, Efexpay, Mikaapp, Palomma, Masu, Somosmekan, Auba, Arkham, Aloi, Liloshop, Getbuo, Nodalnet, Flip-Flow, Zenode.

When you're starting a company, look beyond quick wins. Some of the most transformative businesses tackle fundamental challenges in industries like logistics, infrastructure, and finance. These aren't glamorous sectors, but they're the backbone of economic growth, especially in developing markets. Your success as a founder comes down to two critical things: deep knowledge and genuine passion. The most compelling startups emerge from founders who truly understand their industry's complexities. It's not just about having a good idea—it's about living and breathing the problem you're trying to solve. Networking isn't just a buzzword—it's your lifeline. The connections you build can make or break your startup. Seek out mentors who've been where you want to go, investors who understand your vision, and advisors who aren't afraid to give tough love. These relationships are your secret weapon. Resilience isn't optional—it's everything. Every successful founder has a graveyard of failed ideas and painful pivots. The ones who make it aren't necessarily the smartest, but those who can absorb punches and keep moving forward.

Investing isn't about chasing the hottest trend. It's about identifying solutions to real, persistent problems. A specialized approach lets you develop razor-sharp insights that others miss. Take a specific sector or geographic corridor and become the go-to expert. The best investment is in people, not just numbers. Your role isn't just to provide capital—it's to be a true partner. Show up for founders. Offer strategic guidance. Be the person they can call when things get tough. Think decades, not quarters. Short-term gains are nice, but transformative investments require patience and a commitment to sustainable growth. Structure your deals and relationships with long-term trust and mutual success in mind. Meaningful problems trump trendy solutions every time. The startups that change the world aren't the ones riding a wave of hype, but those quietly solving critical challenges that impact people's lives and industries. The bottom line? Whether you're a founder or an investor, success is about depth, authenticity, and a genuine commitment to creating real value.

In foundational industries,
fall in love with the problem's
complexity, not your solution's
elegance. True B2B innovation
reimagines entire technological
paradigms by solving systemic
challenges that demand deep
domain expertise and pioneering
technical insight.

— Maria Gutierrez Peñaloza

Martha Hernández

Co-Founder and CEO

ESO VENTURES

Oakland, California

$18 million AUM

Martha Hernández is a dynamic serial entrepreneur and CEO and co-founder of ESO Ventures, an organization dedicated to empowering Black, Latino and underinvested entrepreneurs by providing the Confidence, Competence, Capital, Culture and Community needed to thrive. She is also the founder of madeBOS, Inc., a tech-enabled human resources (HR) solution that makes human resources accessible and affordable for small and growing businesses. An Oakland native and product of Oakland Unified School District (OUSD), Martha's deep connection to her community drives her mission to create pathways for underrepresented talent. She earned a bachelor's degree in sociology and Spanish literature from Occidental College in Los Angeles, California, and is a graduate of prestigious leadership programs, including the Mills College Institute for Civic Leadership, Management Leadership for Tomorrow, Coro Fellows Program in Public Affairs, and the Camelback Fellows Program. She further advanced her expertise with certifications in artificial intelligence (AI) business strategy from Massachusetts Institute of Technology (MIT), financial accounting from Harvard Business School, and business scaling from Stanford Business School. Martha is a senior certified professional in human resources from the Society for Human Resource

Management (SHRM-SCP) and serves on the National Small Business Association (NSBA) Leadership Council, where she was also a nominee for the Advocate of the Year Award. Martha serves on the Advisory Board of ReWork the Bay, an initiative of the San Francisco Foundation focused on building an equitable and inclusive economy in the Bay Area and in the Bloomberg American Sustainable Cities initiative for the City of Oakland. In addition to her entrepreneurial endeavors, Martha is a best-selling author. Her book, *I Have What it Takes*, combines powerful stories and actionable principles to inspire leadership among underrepresented and under-resourced individuals. Beyond business, Martha is passionate about fitness and music. Known by her stage name Martha Soledad, she released her debut album, *Prefiero Mandar en Falda*, featuring her original corrido, which champions gender equity and political action. She enjoys spending time with her son, Joaquin, and staying active through boxing and CrossFit.

At ESO Ventures, our investment thesis centers on empowering underinvested entrepreneurs. We aim to address systemic barriers that exclude Black, Latino, female and other disadvantaged entrepreneurs from mainstream financial systems, leveraging innovative practices to democratize entrepreneurship and drive sustainable economic growth. Core components of our investment thesis are: 1. Democratizing Access to Entrepreneurship: We deliver free, high-quality incubator programs and tailored business services, removing barriers to entry and fostering entrepreneurial success through skill-building and access to resources. 2. Innovative Funding Practices: Our progressive lending philosophy ensures that entrepreneurs receive the funding they need while balancing financial accountability. By focusing on relationship-building and alternative metrics like global debt service coverage ratio (GDSCR) and industry-specific ratios, we provide unsecured loans with affordable terms that meet the unique needs of our borrowers. 3. Supporting Entrepreneurs from Underinvested Communities: With over 500 entrepreneurs served, our programs empower businesses led by individuals from historically marginalized groups, including the formerly incarcerated. This focus allows us to target communities most in need of financial empowerment and entrepreneurial support. 4. Creating Sustainable Impact: We emphasize outcomes that benefit both the entrepreneurs and their communities. Our $5.2 million in deployed capital has generated over $10 million in total portfolio revenue, with businesses averaging $115,000 in

revenue. These results showcase the tangible economic transformation our model fosters.
5. High Accountability with Low Risk: Our lending practices result in over 60 percent on time repayments, a 1.9 percent delinquency rate, and zero write-offs, demonstrating the efficacy of our balanced approach to lending.
6. Expanding Our Proven Model Nationally: Our success in California lays the foundation for replicating this model in new markets. With a 9.2 Net Promoter Score reflecting deep trust and satisfaction, we are poised to scale this approach across the country, partnering with institutions to create shared prosperity for underserved communities.

Mother's Touch, Black Latnern Media, Cook & Run, Karl Marie

1. Build with Purpose, Scale with Discipline: Don't just start a business—build a legacy. Understand the "why" behind your venture and align your actions with that purpose. But remember, passion alone isn't enough. Scaling requires discipline—whether it's managing costs, implementing systems, or staying accountable to your mission. The balance between purpose and operational excellence is where transformative impact happens.

2. Invest in Relationships, Not Just Transactions: Success in entrepreneurship isn't just about

closing deals; it's about building relationships that last. Whether it's your team, your customers, or your partners, focus on trust and mutual respect. People support what they help create, so involve your community in your vision. A strong network of collaborators will carry you through challenges and amplify your success.

Your success is not just about what you build but who you uplift along the way. Entrepreneurship is a tool for transformation—use it wisely.

— Martha Hernández

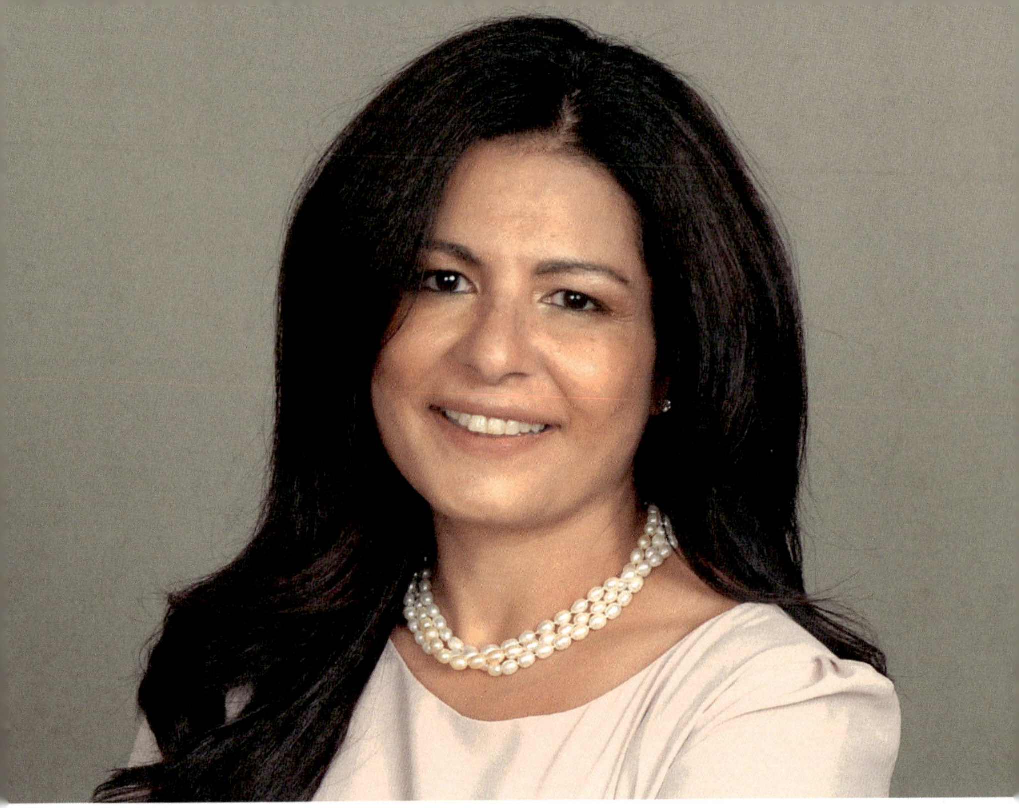

Jennifer
Jeronimo

CEO of Gaingels Inc.

New York

$900 million+ AUM

Jennifer Jeronimo is the CEO of Gaingels, Inc., bringing over twenty years of extensive experience in finance and banking, with key roles at Credit Suisse, Bear Stearns, and JP Morgan, where she rose to executive director. Since joining Gaingels in 2021, Jennifer has championed equitable access and representation in venture capital, demonstrating its positive impact on all stakeholders. Her expertise spans local and global markets, having managed institutional and hedge fund clients and delivered operational efficiencies that saved millions annually while enhancing client experience. At Gaingels, she has built a scalable operation supporting over 2,500 portfolio companies, with $900 million in network investments and a membership exceeding 4,000. Jennifer actively runs deals and launched the Women Achieving Venture Equality (WAVE) program, empowering over 200 women in venture capital over two years. An advocate for underrepresented founders, she serves on the advisory board for Bridge 2 Technologies (B2T) and is dedicated to fostering the next generation of business leaders. Outside of work, Jennifer is an award-winning athlete, a proud mother, and resides in New York City.

- Industry and stage agnostic, but must be venture backed.
- We have invested into over 2,000+ companies examples include 8Sleep, Fireside, Jackpocket (now exited), Digital Robotics.
- If you are looking for fundraising, go to VCs that specialize in what you do and not necessarily just for the "big fish."
- Look for great founders that show grit.

Gaingels mission: "On a mission to show the world that equity of access and representation leads to positive returns."

— Jennifer Jeronimo

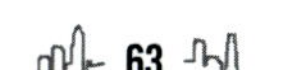

Veronica
Juarez

Managing Partner

DAHLIA VC

Houston, Texas

$15 million AUM

Veronica Juarez is the managing partner of Dahlia VC, a venture capital firm founded to leverage the Latino tech market. Veronica is a seasoned Silicon Valley tech executive with experience building public policy and enterprise teams from the startup to post-initial public offering (IPO) phase. Prior to tech, Veronica spent a decade in politics, working at the federal, state, and local levels for policymakers, working on behalf of their commitment to criminal justice reform, immigration reform, and the arts. Veronica founded Arturo Advisory in 2021, an advisory that works on behalf of funds, companies, and projects that are addressing our world's largest societal inequities. Veronica is a fifth-generation Mexican-American, an honors graduate of Phillips Exeter Academy, and a first-generation college graduate with an honors degree in Comparative Studies in Race & Ethnicity from Stanford University. Stanford awarded her the James W. Lyons Award for Service and the JE Wallace Sterling Book Award for her exceptional leadership, service, and contributions to the university. Fast Company Magazine named her one of the Most Creative People in Business, and The Stanford Alumni Society named her an executive to watch. Veronica manages the grant-giving of The Juarez Family Foundation, a social impact fund she founded in 2019. Veronica serves on the board of Stanford's Center for Comparative Studies in Race and Ethnicity, as a director of Phillips Exeter Academy's General Alumni Association Board, and as the class president for the Class of 2000. Veronica is an active member of Stanford University's First Principles Forum, an intimate invite-only organization dedicated to innovation in philanthropy and social impact. Veronica is a proud native Houstonian, home of her family's infamous taqueria, Villa Arcos, in the 2nd Ward, and enjoys outdoor activities with her puppy, Reggie.

Dahlia VC is a $15-million fund investing in twenty seed stage B2B software as a service (SaaS) and marketplace companies whose success is tied to the growth and economic prosperity of the US Latino population. Latinos are 1 in every 5 Americans starting new businesses at twice the rate of the US population, with ample opportunity as tech consumers. As leaders in those communities, we believe there is a massive opportunity to inject capital into companies serving the Latino cohort, which has historically been overlooked by capital markets.

*Angel Portfolio Includes Journey, Ethos (fund), Bonsai, ShearShare, Public, Rain, LitPic, and Clarity Value

We must never forget what a privilege it is to sit in an investors seat and the responsibility that comes with that privilege.

> It is your own personal evolution that will deliver your company's evolution and success. You have to welcome people's contributions to you and have the courage to meet a new version of yourself at every stage of your growth.
>
> — *Veronica Juarez*

Staci
LaToison

General Partner

Houston, Texas

$1 million+ AUM

Staci LaToison is an award-winning investor, podcaster, speaker, consultant, author, and founder of Dream Big Ventures, a WBENC- and NMSDC-certified women- and minority owned global consulting and professional services firm. Leveraging 22 years of international leadership at Chevron—where she managed global teams and billion-dollar budgets across five continents, including expat assignments in China and Angola—Staci now partners with corporate clients and government agencies to deliver winning, innovative solutions.

Through her podcast *Her Money Moves* and Her Money Moves Summits, Staci demystifies the financial world, inspiring women to take control of their professional careers, financial futures, and build generational wealth. She invests in women-led and diverse-led startups, hosts empowering workshops, and fosters a vibrant community dedicated to encouraging women and girls to dream bigger.

Staci also leads impactful initiatives through her nonprofit, the Dreamgirls Foundation, which is dedicated to mobilizing women and youth through entrepreneurship, financial literacy, and community-building efforts.

Her accomplishments include being honored with "Staci LaToison Day" in

Houston and Her Money Moves Day in Harris County. Staci was named the 2025 Woman of Distinction by the Coastal Bend Women Lawyers Association and 2025 Global Business Innovation Icon by the Ecuadorian-American Chamber of Commerce of Texas. She was recognized as one of 2024's Top 30 Influential Women in Houston and one of the Most Influential Latinas by Latino Leaders Magazine. She received the Mendoza Ventures' Funder of the Year, L'ATTITUDE Ventures Game Changer Award, the Chase Latina Executive Achievement Award, and the Houston Business Journal Women Who Mean Business in Energy Award.

A proud Latina and single mother of two, Staci has been featured in Forbes and Nasdaq and was selected for Finland's prestigious 90 Day Finn Program and the prestigious USGLC Next Gen Global Leaders Network. She serves on several boards, including the University of Houston, Angeles Investors, Houston Hospice, and Discovery Green Conservancy. Staci is also a member of the Latino Corporate Directors Association and Women Presidents Organization.

Our mission is to empower future generations through strategic investments that drive innovation, equity, and generational wealth. We focus on creating transformative impact by supporting businesses, founders, and initiatives that align with our core values of resilience, diversity, and sustainability.

Angeles Ventures Fund I, Mendoza Ventures Inclusion Fund, Portfolia Food and AgTech Fund, Urban Capital Network Horizon Fund I, Softeq Fund I, Agility Bank, Neurable, Mural, Teneral Cellars, Grand Reserve Inn, SpecsX, real estate, short and long-term rentals, stocks/mutual funds

Dream bigger and believe in the power of your unique perspective. The obstacles you face are not barriers—they're stepping stones. Invest in yourself relentlessly and surround yourself with people who challenge and uplift you. Remember, your voice matters, and your ideas have the potential to change the world. Be fearless in taking that first step and unapologetic in your pursuit of success. In an industry full of distractions, stay laser-focused on what truly matters: building a successful product or service that delivers value, generates strong sales, and achieves impactful returns for your employees and investors. Keep your eyes on the end goal, and let every decision reflect your commitment to creating lasting impact.

Investing in underrepresented founders is about unlocking exceptional opportunities. These founders bring unmatched resilience, creativity, and insight to solve real-world problems in ways others cannot. The future of innovation lies in diverse perspectives. By funding these bold visionaries, we not only generate strong returns but also create transformative, generational impact that reshapes industries and communities for the better.

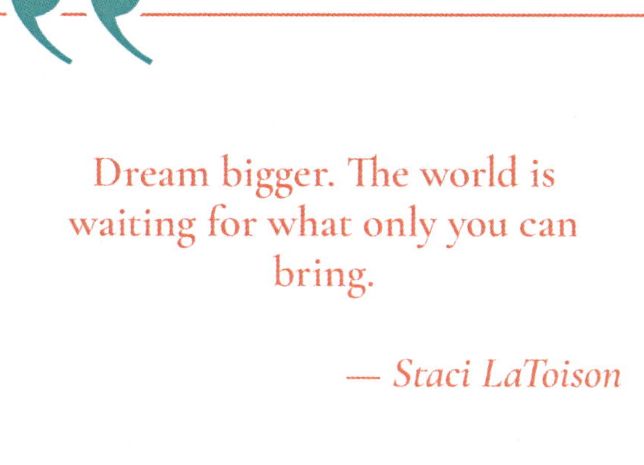

> Dream bigger. The world is waiting for what only you can bring.
>
> — *Staci LaToison*

Macarena
Liu

General Partner

DRIVEN

Santiago, Chile

$7 million AUM

Macarena Liu is a seasoned venture capitalist with over twelve years of experience mentoring, investing in, and scaling startups. As general partner at Driven VC, a seed fund focused on commerce enablers and fintechs across LATAM, she supports founders scaling in Americas' biggest markets: Mexico, Brazil and the United States. She previously led ChileGlobal Ventures' Accelerator, earning it the title of No. 1 accelerator in Chile, supported 100-plus early-stage startups through a pre-seed fund, and oversaw four successful exits. She was also part of the core launch team of Mercado Pago, Mercado Libre's fintech arm, and gained expertise in go-to-market and commercial strategies. Macarena has been recognized as a Top Women Investor by the Latin American Venture Capital Association (LAVCA) in 2022, 2023, and 2024. She is also deeply engaged in women's investment networks, including WeInvest and Global Women in VC, where she works to encourage greater participation of women in the industry through investing, supporting women-led startups, and promoting female representation on boards. Outside work, she's a proud mum of a lively 3 year old and an avid field hockey player, having represented her country in South American and Pan American championships as part of the national field hockey team.

Driven operates a seed fund dedicated to scaling LATAM startups into major markets, including Mexico, Brazil, and the United States. The fund specializes in commerce enablers and fintechs.

Repartes (Chile), Creditop (Colombia), Wareclouds (Chile)

Being an entrepreneur is both incredibly rewarding and undeniably exhausting. Make sure to have a partner who complements your strengths, seek diversity to broaden your perspective, and invest in your mental well-being. For entrepreneurs who are also mothers, I often remind myself: I'm navigating the toughest challenge of all—being a mum. After that, you're unstoppable.

Don't expect success from day one. It takes hard work—there are no easy ways or shortcuts. You'll face hundreds of "nos" before you get to a "yes," but those "nos" are valuable. They'll give you insights to improve your value proposition and help you stand out. Take every "no" as a chance to learn, try to turn them into "yeses," and if you can't, just keep going. Success comes from the "drive." And remember, success is often built with others. Take a collaborative approach—women help other women. Leverage your connections, and use the support around you strategically.

In an industry that is predominantly male, you either need to find your way in or pave your own path.

— Macarena Liu

Karla
Magana Figueroa

Senior Investment Manager

CANDIDE GROUP

San Francisco, California

$250 million AUM

Karla Magana Figueroa (she/ella) brings a decade of experience driving strategic decisions at the intersection of finance and public policy. At Candide, she is responsible for impact investment strategies across various asset classes and stages, all in service of creating a more equitable economy. Prior to Candide, Karla ran due diligence on marquee technology transactions on JP Morgan's technology coverage group in the investment banking division. Karla also has extensive exposure to philanthropic and racial justice work, advising organizations such as the Bloomberg Harvard City Leadership Initiative and LinkedIn's Global Impact team. Karla received a master of business administration and a master of public policy from the University of Chicago Booth School of Business and the Harvard Kennedy School, respectively. She is a formerly undocumented immigrant and the proud daughter of a Mexican migrant farm worker. A longstanding equity advocate, her experience includes leading the Junior Leadership Board of Sponsors for Educational Opportunity (SEO) and serving on the Investment Committee of the Cap Table Coalition. For her contributions to marginalized communities and promising career trajectory, Karla has been identified as a Rising Star through the Most Powerful Latinas Summit hosted by the Association of Latino Professionals for America (ALPFA). In her free time, Karla likes to read long-form journalism pieces, roller skate around the Bay Area, and scope out the best taco in any city.

Candide Group works with families, foundations, and other investors who believe that finance can serve as a tool of empowerment rather than a weapon of extraction. As a registered investment advisor, we focus on private assets—debt, private equity, real assets, and innovative new structures—where there are both real capital needs and opportunities for mission-aligned investors to build impactful portfolios.

Cherryrock Capital, Impact America Fund, Solar Holler, Westbound Equity Partners, and Dirt Capital Partners

Seek investors who share your values and can amplify your mission through their networks.

Focus on capitalizing solutions that address the root causes of systemic challenges for lasting impact.

I tell my students, 'When you get these jobs that you have been so brilliantly trained for, just remember that your real job is that if you are free, you need to free somebody else. If you have some power, then your job is to empower somebody else.'

— *Toni Morrison*

Bianca Martinelli

Partner

ALEXIA VENTURES

São Paulo

$83 million AUM

Before joining Alexia Ventures, Bianca spent 12 years at Endeavor, where she helped build entrepreneurial ecosystems across 40+ countries. She led the organization's global operations and spearheaded its expansion into Italy, Spain, Peru, and Ecuador.

She later served as Vice President of International Expansion at RD Station, a leading digital marketing and sales platform for small and medium-sized businesses in emerging markets. In this role, she drove the company's entry into Mexico and Colombia.

Bianca holds a bachelor's degree in business administration from FGV EAESP in São Paulo, Brazil, and specialized in entrepreneurship at Columbia Business School. She is also a Kauffman Fellow, a mentor at Endeavor, and a board member at Emerging Venture Capital Fellows (EVCF)."

Alexia VC is an early-stage investor backing top Latin American entrepreneurs who are transforming industries through software and AI-driven business models.

Logcomex, Mecanizou, Lexter, Herospark, Parfin, Finbits, Winnin, Seedz, and Rocket. Chat

Embrace the complexities of your market as opportunities for differentiation. Your deep understanding of local challenges can be a significant advantage in creating innovative solutions that stand out. Leverage this insight to build strategies that not only address local needs but also have the potential to scale internationally.

Investing in early-stage ventures means betting on people first. Take the time to deeply understand the founders' vision, resilience, and abilities to adapt. In emerging markets, where challenges often require creative solutions, identifying founders with grit and a clear mission can make all the difference in the success of your investments.

Your boldness is part of the solution to transform the future. By embracing your true identity and accepting your uniqueness, you become an inspiration to others.

— Bianca Martinelli

Laura I. Maydón

Founder and Partner

ascendO Venture Capital

Miami

$50 million AUM

Laura I. Maydón is the founder of Ascendo, a venture capital firm unlocking trillions of dollars of untapped, overlooked opportunities nationwide. She brings experience as founder, operator and investor. Prior to Ascendo, Laura founded Endeavor Miami in 2013, the first US affiliate of the global entrepreneurial organization, pioneering Miami's entrepreneurial hub. During that time, Laura built a portfolio of more than twenty companies generating over $250 million in revenues, several with substantial exits. Prior to Endeavor, she held leadership positions at Visa and Panamco. Laura has strong fintech, mergers and acquisitions, and private equity experience. Laura serves on the board of NASDAQ: IMXI and as a member of the Investment Committee of Salkantay Ventures. In addition, she volunteers as a member of NWS Digital Committee and as Vice-Chair of the HBS Women's Student Association Alumnae Board. Laura has a Master of Business Administration from Harvard Business School and a Bachelor of Science degree in Economics (Summa Cum Laude) from Instituto Tecnológico Autónomo de México (ITAM) in Mexico City.

Ascendo is a venture capital firm unlocking trillions of dollars of untapped opportunities nationwide that are currently overlooked. Using a first-principles approach, we invest in groundbreaking founders, leveraging diversity in the pursuit of alpha. We capitalize on the convergence of rapid technological advancement and shifting demographics by investing in disruptive early-stage companies that address the needs of growing demographic segments, as well as empower women as catalysts of economic growth. We have a preference for fintech, edtech, future of work, healthtech and enterprise software. The venture funding gap represents an asymmetric market opportunity and diverse founders are best positioned to address the growing market needs. What is our edge? Our unique skillset combines cultural trust-building, founder-investor synergy, and disciplined execution to access differentiated deal-flow and execute our strategy. Beyond capital, we provide an ecosystem of resources to help founders scale faster.

Suma Wealth and LeapFinancial

Lead with purpose: The founder's journey is never linear. If you're going to invest your energy and effort, choose something deeply aligned with your values that will sustain you through the highs and lows.

Balance intuition with data: Founders who adapt quickly to market shifts while staying true to their purpose are more likely to succeed. Use data to guide you, but trust your instincts when it matters. Don't lose sight of true value creation. It is the foundation for solid unit economics and long-term success.

Community is an asset: Be intentional about connecting with investors, founders, and business leaders early-on.

Ask for help: The founder journey can be isolating. Cultivate relationships with mentors who encourage your growth and investors who bring strategic value beyond capital.

Define your vision for growth: Have clarity on the type of business you want to build. If your goal is to scale fast and to pursue venture funding, understand how it accelerates growth while evolving ownership dynamics over time.

Build for lasting impact: You can have a lasting difference in our community and achieve financial success.

Enjoy the journey! Celebrate early wins and embrace challenges as an opportunity for growth.

These are the things that I strive to do well.

Invest with purpose: Alignment with our true purpose fuels transformation. Purpose-driven investments have the power to deliver both strong returns and lasting impact. We have the power to transform our industry!

Define your unique view: Stay curious and adaptive. Hold conviction in your investment thesis, even if it challenges wisdom. Contrarian views often lead to greatest breakthroughs.

Fuel innovation through inclusion: Expand your lenses. Diversity in all its forms drives innovation, unlocks untapped markets that others overlook and creates a path for higher returns. It's the right thing to do AND a smart business advantage.

Be a strategic partner: Go beyond executing deals. True value comes from providing founders with the resources, guidance, and networks they need to accelerate growth and to drive to successful exits.

Foster collaboration: Together we can transform our industry. Build meaningful connections and intentionally reach beyond your immediate circle. By fostering collaboration, we can grow an inclusive ecosystem that drives a win-win economy for all stakeholders.

Celebrate with founders: Enjoy the journey! Take time to celebrate and acknowledge the resilience that founders have to succeed.

I envision a future where innovation knows no bounds and opportunity is accessible to all. Ascendo is my contribution to building a lasting investment platform that fuels an inclusive economy. This will be achieved by backing founders who challenge the status quo, rewriting the rules, and shaping the world for generations—all while pursuing superior returns.

— Laura I. Maydón

Samara
Mejia Hernandez

Founding Partner

chingona ventures

Chicago, Illinois

$60 million AUM

The firm is run by Samara Mejia Hernandez, who has spent over nineteen years selling, advising, and investing in the public and private markets. Her venture experience spans across four funds with over 100 investments made.

Chingona Ventures is an early-stage venture capital firm in Chicago that leads investments in US-based software startups that redefine how we live, work, learn and earn. We invest early and are often the largest check in a company's first institutional round. We back founders across the country that are well positioned to create businesses in undercapitalized growth markets and to take advantage of the demographic shifts that are redefining our world. We look for the "Chingona Factor" in founders—the grit to take the leap and courage to do things their own way.

We currently have invested in thrity nine companies and you can learn more on our website about our great companies.

You will get so many people telling you "no." Focus on getting your first "yes." You only need a few first believers (customers, employees, investors) to get started.

Dare to invest differently.

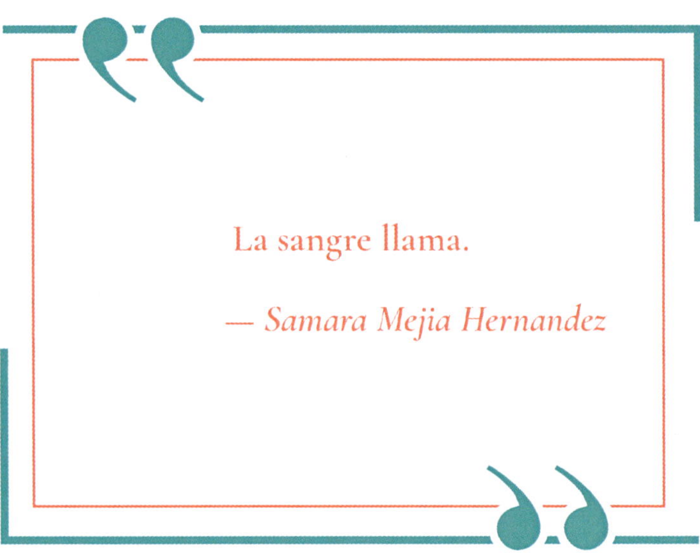
La sangre llama.
— *Samara Mejia Hernandez*

Ana Carolina Mexia Ponce

Co-founding Partner

NIDO VENTURES

San Francisco, California

$7 million AUM

Ana Carolina Mexia Ponce is the co-founder and managing partner at Nido Ventures, a venture capital fund investing in pre-seed and seed companies transforming foundational industries in the United States - Mexico corridor. A Forbes 30 Under 30 honoree, she has guided Nido Ventures to secure support from notable investors - including Bill Gates' daughter, Jennifer Gates - and achieved significant portfolio growth within its first two years. Born and raised in Mexico City, Ana Carolina brings a strong technical perspective to her role as an investor. Her background in software engineering, combined with her business acumen, enables her to evaluate and nurture innovative technologies effectively. Before founding Nido Ventures, she gained industry experience through roles at LinkedIn and Siclo, a Mexican fitness company. Ana Carolina holds a bachelor of science degree in computer science and a master in business administration from Stanford University. This blend of technical knowledge and strategic business skills positions her uniquely in the venture capital landscape, particularly in identifying and supporting promising B2B technologies.

Pre-Seed & Seed companies transforming traditional industries in the United States - Mexico corridor

Arkham, Flipzen, Auba, Zenode, and Nodal Networks

Your cap table represents more than equity percentages—it's a roster of believers, builders, and partners invested in your vision. Treat it with intentionality and respect. Every name represents someone who took a chance on your company, whether through capital, talent, or guidance. When managed thoughtfully, your cap table becomes a foundation for lasting relationships and aligned incentives.

VC is an asset class that allows for creativity, so bring your own flavor to it.

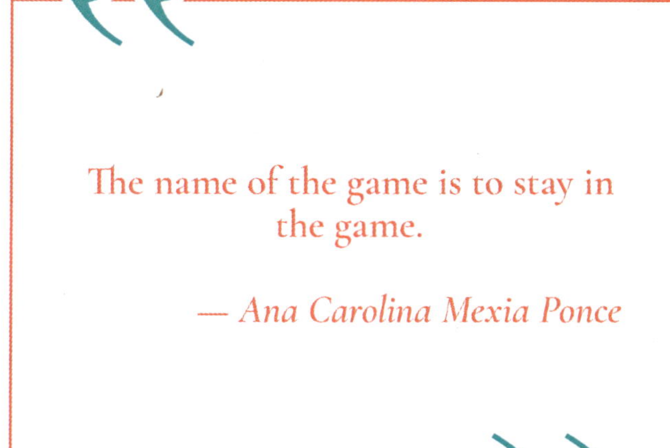

The name of the game is to stay in the game.

— Ana Carolina Mexia Ponce

Stephanie Michael Silva

Partner and Co-Founder

libra LEADERS

Mexico City, Mexico

Targeting $50 million AUM

Stephanie Michael Silva is a Chilean-American with a decade of investment experience across public and private markets. She has also driven strategic initiatives at startups. She started her career in Equity Research at Citigroup covering financials stocks, then pivoted to global Private Equity at MLC Australia, co-investing directly into ten companies across the United States and Europe in the fintech, B2B, SaaS, and healthcare sectors, as well as invested in the best global buyout and VC funds as a Limited Partner. In her career in VC, Stephanie has focused on the United States and LATAM, having lived and worked in Mexico and Brazil. She has held roles at L'ATTITUDE Ventures, Gilgamesh Ventures, 1616 Ventures and Digital Currency Group. Stephanie has maintained her focus on fintech and AI as an investor and in her work with startups. She wrote her Master's thesis on the "Role of Regulation in the Growth of the Fintech Ecosystems in Brazil versus Mexico" and has aided fintech and AI startups in the United States and LATAM in international expansion strategy, partnerships, GTM, fundraising and financial modeling. She received her MBA and Master of Arts in International Studies from The Wharton School and The Lauder Institute at the University of Pennsylvania and her Bachelor of Science in Business Administration and Bachelor of Arts in Public Policy from The University of North Carolina at Chapel Hill.

Libra Leaders invests in the best early-stage tech founders in the Americas.

Comp, Neofin, Exabeam, Unanet, Finantix

Find and build authentic relationships with the investors who truly understand your vision and are aligned with your mission—fundraising is about more than capital; it's about finding the right partners for your journey.

Backing women and diverse founders unlocks innovation and access to underserved markets, driving the kind of outsized returns that redefine success in venture capital.

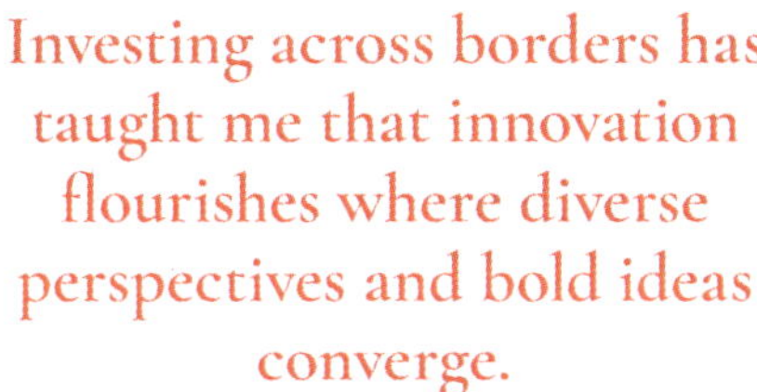

Investing across borders has taught me that innovation flourishes where diverse perspectives and bold ideas converge.

— Stephanie Michael Silva

Lisa Morales-Hellebo

Founder and Managing General Partner

RE
FASH
IOND

New York, New York

$3.3 million AUM

Lisa Morales-Hellebo has thirty years of experience in tech, design and systems thinking, entrepreneurship, and community building. She has recently added VC to her list of titles as Founder and Managing General Partner at REFASHIOND Ventures: The Industrial Transformation Fund — a New York-based venture fund that invests as the first institutional check in early-stage startups refashioning industrial value chains to be better for people, the planet, and profits, across Data and AI, Advanced Materials, Advanced Manufacturing, and Next-Generation Supply Chains, defensible through economic moats.

Lisa has always been obsessed with how things are made and pioneered mass customization, personalization, and on-demand micromanufacturing for P&G in Silicon Valley in 1999 at a company called Reflect.com. She is catalyzing the paradigm shift to localized demand chains as CEO and Founder of REFASHIOND OS (rOS), which collaborates with her fund's portfolio companies to facilitate their integration, adoption, and scale via rOS' key initiatives.

Lisa is also a Founder of The Worldwide Supply Chain Federation, an organization that is changing how supply chain professionals learn about, collaborate on, and adopt early-stage supply chain innovation around the world. She is a Carnegie Mellon University alum with University Honors, a Techstars alum, and the Founder of the New York Fashion Tech Lab. She serves on the boards of three other accelerators and has been featured in numerous publications, along with two previous books.

Lisa has received several awards, including Supply & Demand Chain Executive Magazine's Top Woman in Supply Chain 2022, and recognition as one of the Top 100 Women in Supply Chain in 2020, 2021, 2022, and 2023. She was also named one of WWD's Most Influential ESG Leaders in 2023.

REFASHIOND Ventures invests in early-stage companies that are refashioning legacy value chains to be better for people, planet, and profits, across Data and AI, Advanced Materials, Advanced Manufacturing, and Next-Gen Supply Chains.

Advocat, BOPA, Arvist, Kaya, Portex, Wisy

Focus your finite time and energy on people that amplify your work and see your value from the first meeting.

Never follow investment trends. Carve your own lane so you can own your unique deal flow.

I live in the future and prefer to invest in or build innovations that have never existed before.

— Lisa Morales-Hellebo

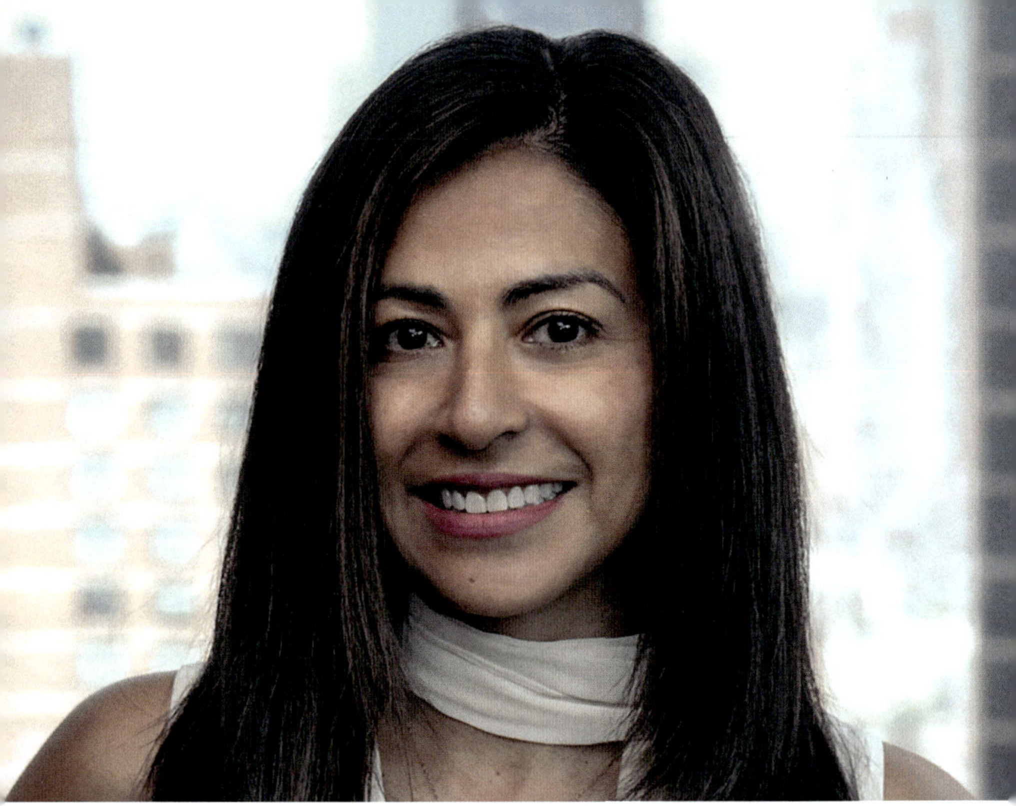

Laura
Moreno Lucas

General Partner

L'ATTITUDE VENTURES

libra LEADERS

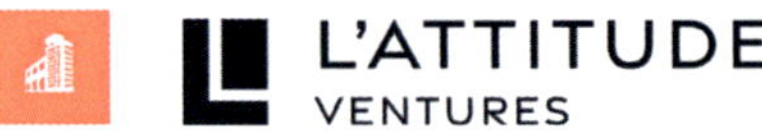

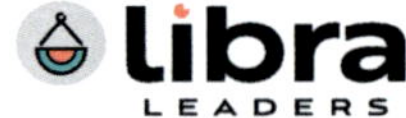

San Francisco, California

$100M AUM

Laura Moreno Lucas is a general partner at L'ATTITUDE Ventures, a $100 million purpose-led venture fund that invests in early-stage US Latino-led and owned businesses. Previously, Laura was the managing director of the Nasdaq, Inc. stock exchange and the founder of Pandocap, a strategic financial advisory services firm, and Ladada, a fashion subscription company. She also mentors at accelerators like Black Ambition and 500 Startups and is on the board of multiple non-profits. In her role at L'ATTITUDE Ventures, she focuses on changing the investment landscape for Latino entrepreneurs. Born in Guadalajara, Mexico, she immigrated to the United States when she was seven years old and understands the challenges confronting Latino entrepreneurs scaling their startups into proper product-market fit and gaining access to capital markets. She recently launched a women's initiative called Libra Leaders, an effort that is tipping the scales of capital towards women. This initiative, centered around a network of visible leaders, is promoting women's entrepreneurship to expand wealth creation, inspiring a new generation of female business leaders.

L'ATTITUDE Ventures is a $100 million venture fund dedicated to investing in early-stage (pre-seed to Series A) US Latina/o entrepreneurs. With 40 percent of our portfolio companies being led by Latinas. US Latinos represent the most entrepreneurial and significant growth cohort in the country, accounting for one in every four new entrepreneurs and 27 percent of net gross domestic product (GDP) growth.

Mavida Health, Caplight, Paladin, Sunthetics, Deepblocks, Flow, Lilu, Omnitron, Novospace, and Nopalera

Being an entrepreneur is incredibly challenging and comes with countless obstacles. It takes character and strength to manage setbacks, pivot when necessary, and continuously learn from mistakes. Remember, this journey is a marathon, not a sprint. As a woman, you bring unique insights and perspectives—trust in that, because it's your competitive edge. Believe in yourself, as confidence inspires confidence in others.

As an investor I try to stay out of the way, and always remember that I am a part of a larger vision. Therefore, guiding and supporting should always be a top priority.

The knowledge you possess should always be shared—it might be the lesson someone else needs to grow.

— *Laura Moreno Lucas*

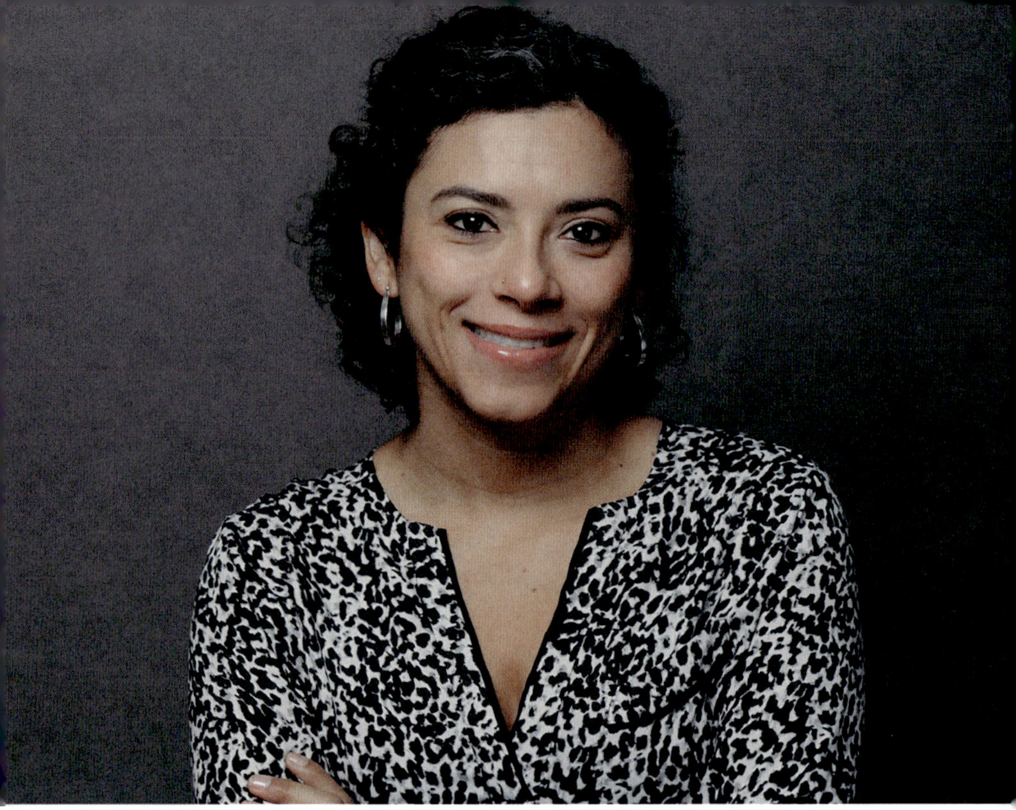

Diana
Narváez

Principal

Brazil

$850 million AUM

With a background as an entrepreneur, investor, operator, and business consultant, Diana Narváez brings a unique breadth of knowledge and experience to her role as a venture capital investor. Having lived in Colombia, Brazil, and Mexico, she is deeply connected to the region and takes a hands-on approach to building relationships with fintech founders in LatAm.

In her role as Flourish's lead investor in LatAm, Diana has expanded the firm's presence across the region, working closely with the founding teams of rising fintechs, such as Kamino, Swap, Banco Neon, Albo, Dolado, Heru, among others. Most recently, she led Flourish's investments in Akua, Morada Uno, and Minu.

Before joining Flourish, Diana oversaw strategy and business development for Pickup, a Colombian motorcycle ride-hailing and last-mile logistics VC-backed startup. Previously, she co-founded and led Impulsa Capital, an impact investing vehicle for family offices in Colombia. There, she fundraised from angel investors globally and developed a portfolio of mission-driven, early-stage companies.

Fluent in Spanish, Portuguese, and English, she has worked in every major economy in Latin America, including stints with McKinsey in Mexico and JPMorgan in Brazil. A strategic advisor to social impact startups, incubators, and industry ecosystem organizations, Diana was part of the co-founding team of what is now the Diversity VC LATAM chapter, an initiative to create a more equitable, diverse, and inclusive VC sector. Diana has a bachelor's degree in accountancy from Northern Illinois University and an MBA degree from Cornell University. She is an alumna of Stanford University's VC Unlocked program, a National Outdoor Leadership School (NOL) outdoor leadership educator and is passionate about adventure travel, rock climbing, mountaineering, and mentoring.

With $850M under management, Flourish Ventures is a global fintech venture capital firm with purpose, backing bold entrepreneurs building companies to disrupt legacy structures and shape financial systems for the better.

The firm's portfolio includes industry leaders such as Chime, Kin, Indifi, M2P, Neon, Hummingbird, Qoala, ShopUp, Swap, and Unit, among other high-growth companies.

Funding: Select your investors wisely. The best investors are partners who challenge, support, grow with you, and genuinely understand and share your long-term vision. Great investors bring more than money.

Look for those who offer strategic guidance, industry expertise, and valuable networks. Evaluate their track record and speak to other founders they've backed to understand their approach, involvement, and reputation. Foster transparent and regular communication from the start. Keeping investors informed builds trust and enables them to provide timely, relevant advice. Resilience and Wellbeing: Founder wellbeing is a critical component of startup success. There is a strong correlation between founder wellbeing and startup performance. A founder's physical, mental, and emotional health directly impacts their ability to lead effectively, make sound decisions, and sustain focus during the high-pressure journey of building a startup. When challenges arise, focus on what you can control: your mission, your customers, and the value you create. Reframe setbacks as opportunities to innovate using first principles thinking. Build a supportive team culture with open communication and shared wins. Set boundaries to avoid burnout, and don't hesitate to ask for help or delegate. Resilience isn't just about surviving tough times; it's about thriving through learning, adapting, and staying committed to your vision.

$ As an investor, our role extends beyond providing capital—we have the power to shape a founder's journey. By fostering stability, demonstrating empathy, and building true partnerships, investors can profoundly influence a founder's ability to succeed. Startups inevitably face challenges and founders need investors who provide constructive support instead of adding pressure. Investors could help founders prioritize and break problems into manageable steps, while reassuring them that setbacks are a natural part of growth. Believing in their capabilities can reignite their confidence and focus. Healthy founders build thriving companies. For this reason, investors can add value to founders by advocating for their well-being by promoting sustainable work practices, offering mentorship, and fostering a safe environment for learning from mistakes. Ultimately, investors should invest in people, not just ideas. Seek out founders who are resilient, adaptable, and mission-driven. With patience, empathy, and a focus on impact, investors can help create lasting and meaningful change.

It's an exciting time to be in venture capital—a sector with the potential to unlock LATAM's innovation, empower transformative startups, and tackle the region's most pressing challenges with impactful solutions.

— *Diana Narváez*

Cristina
Nuñez

Co-founder and Managing Partner

True Beauty Ventures

Miami, Florida, and New York, New York

$117 million AUM

Cristina Nuñez has spent the last seventeen years advising, investing, and operating in the consumer products industry. After focusing the last ten years on beauty and wellness, Cristina co-founded True Beauty Ventures alongside her partner, Rich Gersten, with the purpose of addressing a white space investment opportunity as indie beauty brands had limited access to strategic capital with true expertise and checks less than $5 million. Cristina is dedicated to building emerging beauty and wellness indie brands into enduring brands of scale by leveraging her unique investing and operating experience, insider beauty network and vast industry knowledge. Nuñez currently sits on the board of category-leading and defining brands, including Maude, modern sexual wellness and intimacy brand; Youthforia, a clean makeup brand; Crown Affair, clean, ritualistic hair care brand; Caliray, a California-inspired clean and sustainable beauty brand; Moon Juice, adaptogenic beauty and wellness brand; Iris&Romeo, a clean makeup-skincare hybrid; and Feals, a mental health-focused cannabidiol brand. As a proud first-generation Cuban American, Cristina is also dedicated to sourcing, investing, and supporting Black, Indigenous, and people of color (BIPOC) founded and focused brands that lead with integrity, empathy, and strong values. Her strong contributions to the beauty ecosystem have garnered industry recognition, including being named one of 2023's Most Inspirational Women Leaders by WWD and featured in Latino Leaders' 100 Latinas of 2023 List. She is also consistently featured in leading beauty publications, such as Beauty Independent, Beauty Matter, Business of Fashion, and Glossy for her industry perspective. Prior to True Beauty Ventures, Cristina held key operational roles within the beauty and wellness industry. She served as general manager and chief operating officer at Clark's Botanicals, a clean botanical skincare brand, where she developed marketing and product strategies and managed operational and financial performance. Before that, she held multiple senior positions at Laura Geller Beauty, a prestige makeup brand, including chief of staff, executive director of global strategy and business development, and director of project management and operations. Cristina also worked on developing strategic business initiatives and growth opportunities for Equinox, a luxury fitness and lifestyle brand. Cristina started her professional career in finance, where she focused on consumer products and retail. She was a senior associate at private equity firm Tengram Capital Partners, where she made investments in middle market consumer brands. Prior to that, she was an associate at L Catterton, the largest consumer focused private equity fund. She began her career as an analyst in the Consumer & Retail Investment Banking Group at UBS. Cristina graduated magna cum laude from Duke University and holds a bachelor in arts degree with highest distinction in public policy studies and political science.

True Beauty Ventures pursues investments in emerging growth beauty and wellness brands leveraging decades of sector expertise, knowledge, and network. The partners' extensive beauty investing and operating experience allows them to identify winning brands at an inflection point of breakout growth and help them scale and exit successfully. As sector specialists, True Beauty has the flexibility to invest across multiple growth stages, from Seed to Series C.

True Beauty Ventures' investments include K18 Hair (exited), Caliray, Crown Affair, Maude, Vacation, Moon Juice, Dieux Skin, The 7 Virtues, Ami Cole, Sofie Pavitt, Cay Skin, Feals, Kinship, BeautyStat, The Maker, Youthforia, evolvetogether, and Iris&Romeo.

- Prioritize what's most important. The phrase "first things first" exists for a reason. Focus and prioritization are the keys to startup success.

- Fail fast, learn faster. Inevitably you will fail at some point. Deliberately use failure to drive success.

Don't find the fault. Find the fix. Instead of focusing on identifying what's wrong with a situation or problem (the non-diverse VC landscape, the inequities in fundraising, the glass ceiling, etc.) actively look for solutions and ways to improve it. Prioritize finding a remedy rather than dwelling on the blame.

— *Cristina Nuñez*

Ana Quintana

Managing Partner

BLACK DIAMOND VENTURES

Los Angeles, California

$250 million AUM

Ana Quintana, a tech-driven investor and entrepreneur, brings over twenty-five years of experience in venture capital, tech startups, and investment operations. Her keen ability to identify early-stage growth opportunities and cultivate valuable partnerships is essential to BDV, its founders, and portfolio companies, and LPs. As BDV's managing partner, Ana recently led and launched an opportunity fund strategically designed to invest in innovative and diverse founders developing transformative technologies alongside leading VCs. The fund's focus and strategy offer a level of agility and access to emerging biotech and deep tech companies throughout its Series A, B, and growth stages. Ana serves on the board of several BDV portfolio companies, including Alveo Technologies, Ares Materials, Engage3, and MuMo. Ana is also active in the local tech community as a committee member and a founding member of SHE Ventures in Tech, a group that offers entrepreneurial support to female founders.

We invest in transformative and emerging verticals in AI, machine learning (ML), big data, materials science, and semiconductors within the biotech and deep-tech sectors, typically at Series A, B and follow on, optimizing the balance of risk with the goal of delivering accelerated capital returns to LPs.

Altwork, ALVEO, Ares Materials, Engage3, MUMO, Strateos

Find what you're most passionate about, seek advice, mentorship, authenticity, and embrace fortitude and grace when your energy calls for it.

Relationships that develop into true partnerships are invaluable and key.

Fostering a positive and measurable impact within our emerging and diverse entrepreneurial ecosystem is crucial for meaningful opportunities, growth, and a successful future in venture.

— *Ana Quintana*

Miriam
Rivera

CEO, Co-Founder & Managing Director

ULU VENTURES

Palo Alto, CA

$400M+ AUM

Miriam Rivera is CEO, Co-Founder and Managing Director of Ulu Ventures, a top-tier seed stage venture capital (VC) firm based in Silicon Valley focused on high-growth and market-leading information technology and internet companies. The firm was founded in 2008 and has more than $400M in assets under management, 10 unicorns in its portfolio, including two US public companies, Palantir and SoFi. Ulu was the first Latina-led venture fund in Silicon Valley and Miriam is a recognized pioneer in the technology and VC communities.

Before co-founding Ulu, Miriam was Vice President and Deputy General Counsel at Google, joining in 2001 as its second attorney. Her work to simplify contracts helped Google scale from $85m to $10b in 5 years. Prior to Google, Miriam was a cofounder of a VC and angel-backed software company along with partner and Ulu co-founder Clint Korver.

Miriam earned AB, AM and JD/MBA degrees from Stanford. One study funded by the Kauffman Foundation determined that Stanford-founded companies would comprise the 10th largest economy in the world, if all the companies created by its alumni were treated as a country. 1 university, 240,000 alumni, the 10th largest economy in the world.

Miriam has been a trustee of Stanford University and was: honored with the Stanford

Medal, awarded to fewer than 1 percent of alumni; elected to the Stanford Multicultural Hall of Fame, which recognizes diverse alumni for their exceptional service to the university and society; and won the Stanford Graduate School of Business Porras Award for Leadership. Miriam is a co-founder and former co-president and board member of Stanford Angels & Entrepreneurs, Stanford's largest alumni club. She served on Stanford Law School's: Venture Fund, Dean's Advisory Council and Board of Visitors; Stanford's Graduate School of Business Dean's Advisory Council; Stanford's Office of Technology Licensing Advisory Board and the advisory committee for Stanford's Diverse Manager Initiative.

In addition she served as a trustee and chair of the Investment Committee for the Kauffman Foundation, a private foundation with $2.6B in assets and was an advisor to the Launch with Goldman Sachs Advisory Council. Currently, she serves on the San Francisco Federal Reserve Bank Economic Advisory Council, Silicon Valley Bank Advisory Board, Acumen Fund America Board of Directors, and Sesame Workshop (Sesame Street). She is a Kauffman Fellow in VC and was a class 15 leadership award winner.

In her free time, she enjoys her two adult daughters, partner, dog and many friends, travel, as well as time in nature. She measures the quality of her life by how many days she spends on the beach, preferably a warm one.

Ulu's mission is to become a premier seed stage venture firm in the US, demonstrating that team diversity and decision analysis drive superior venture returns. Diverse teams are those that include women, people of color, and immigrants alongside whites, men/other genders, and all permutations of such folks on a team. Premier to us means:

- generating consistent, exceptional performance fund-over-fund
- being a catalyst for thousands of diverse entrepreneurial teams over successive generations of Ulu GPs, enabling startup founders to take a shot at changing the world and building wealth for themselves, their communities, the Ulu team, and our Limited Partners
- creating an inclusive, values-aligned community of team members, LPs, entrepreneurs, and co-investors who welcome and challenge each other
- unlocking entrepreneurs' full potential and helping them take smart risks; for those who have the added responsibility of being role models in their communities, this includes creating safety in the event of failure

Through our example of how diversity can drive superior returns, we aspire to dramatically increase investment in diverse entrepreneurs and diverse fund managers across the venture industry so we can improve the US economy, create more jobs, and remain competitive globally. We also aspire to improve decision making in the venture industry by helping the industry use data and analytics to reduce bias and take smart risks.

Ulu has a large number of companies in its portfolio, with 10 unicorns, including two US public companies, Palantir and SoFi. Our portfolio companies are listed on our website at https://uluventures.com/companies/.

I've visited entrepreneurial ecosystems in many parts of the US and nearly as many countries around the world. American entrepreneurship is a beacon of hope and a source of know-how in all countries. It's stunning to see what can be accomplished through investments in entrepreneurial ecosystems. Everywhere you go, people who'd been structurally locked out in the past are being included, because you need talent from every quarter to lift up a nation and engender social stability.

Entrepreneurial production is the economy of the future. We must learn and teach its mindset, technical and technology skills everywhere in the US. There will always be work for entrepreneurship-minded individuals even as whole categories of jobs become obsolete. We are a creative species. Entrepreneurs live to solve problems with hearts, mind, spirit and hands; to make a difference.

Decisions vs. Outcomes

The most important distinction in making better decisions and driving better venture performance is that between making a good decision and receiving a good outcome.

Uncertainty creates a disconnect between good decisions and good outcomes, in that one does not necessarily follow from the other. A good decision is one made in the best possible way given the situation we face. A good outcome is one that we like. Making a good decision is the best we can do, but it does not guarantee a good outcome. Conversely, a bad outcome by itself says nothing about the quality of the decision made.

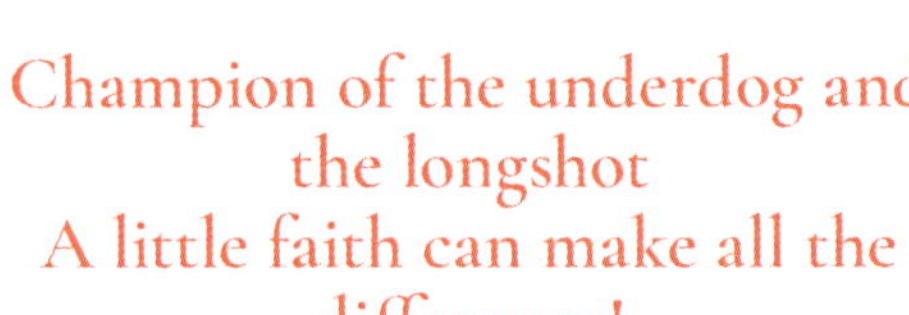

Champion of the underdog and
the longshot
A little faith can make all the
difference!

— Miriam Rivera

Antonia
Rojas

Managing Partner

attom CAPITAL

Mexico City, Mexico

Confidential AUM

Antonia Rojas founded Attom Capital, the first direct secondary fund in Latin America. Before Attom Capital, she has been leading investments in tech companies for the last ten years, being on the board with top-tier investors, such as Lightspeed, Accel, QED and NFX. There were part of her investments in companies like Nuvocargo, Flink, Flat, among others, and as part of being a partner at ALLVP and Manutara Ventures, before launching Attom Capital. Antonia holds a master's degree in social entrepreneurship from Hult International Business School in San Francisco, an undergraduate degree in business and economics from Pontificia Universidad Católica in Chile, and is part of Kauffman Fellows Class 25.

Direct secondary investments in Latin America.

Not Disclosed.

Keep pushing and find ways to build moats to your business early.

Partner with founders who create massive impact and value, but they also find creative ways to capture that value in a sustainable way.

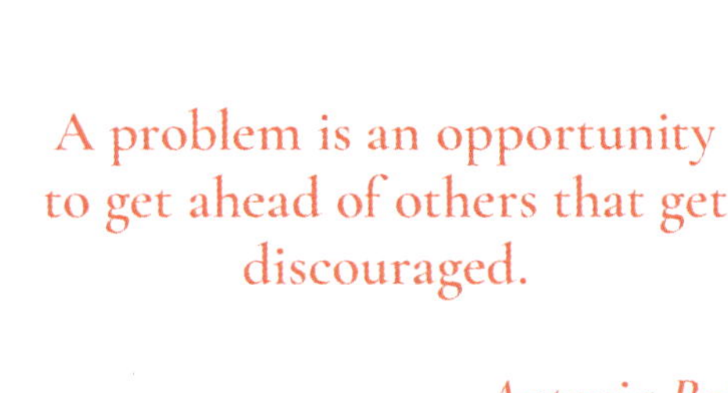

A problem is an opportunity to get ahead of others that get discouraged.

— Antonia Rojas

Ashley
Ryder

Partner

Vamos Ventures

New York, New York

$50 million AUM

Ashley Ryder is a partner at VamosVentures. She started her career at Morgan Stanley in Capital Markets and moved into strategic roles at Y Combinator startup Shoptiques.com (now Material Retail), Saks Fifth Avenue, and Estée Lauder focused on the intersection of the consumer and technology verticals. She was previously an investor at Brand Foundry Ventures, Founders Factory, and Dorm Room Fund across commerce, healthcare, and fintech. Ashley holds a bachelor of arts degree from Brown University and a master in business administration from MIT Sloan. She has received many accolades for her role in the New York City tech community, including Negocios Now's Latinos 40 Under 40 for the Tri-State NYC Area 2024, Forum Ventures' Top NYC Founder-First Investors 2024, NYC Fintech Women's Inspiring Fintech Females 2022, and NextGen's Rising Star VC 2022.

VamosVentures is an early-stage venture capital fund investing in extraordinary diverse tech teams across Pre-Seed to Series A rounds. The fund has a big bet on the Latinx opportunity in the United States and cares about returns and impact. VamosVentures is on a mission to generate market-rate investment returns, and deliver meaningful impact through wealth creation, social mobility, unique tech solutions, and taking a visible and clear stand as diverse investors.

Altera, Ocho, Suma Wealth, Zocalo Health, Galileo, Handspring Health, Culina Health, Clarity Pediatrics, and Yuvo Health.

Stay curious no matter where you are in the founding journey. Constantly ask your customers for feedback on your offering and ways to make it better. You do not need to have a perfect product. Listen, adjust, and repeat until customers cannot live without it.

Being uniquely you is your power as an investor. Embrace that you have a differentiated understanding of problems from your lived experience. This is what makes you able to foster certain connections and invest in the best founders.

"I'm a New York City girl, born and raised in Staten Island. I'm proud of where I'm from. My mother is Puerto Rican from Brooklyn, and my father is an immigrant from Turkey. My mother has spent her entire career at the USPS and my father as a building super. I learned from them an important life lesson—that grit and believing in a better future can bring you a long way. Now, more than ever, this lesson rings true in the world of tech. I'm energized every single day by founders from all backgrounds and experiences wanting to rewrite the way things have been done in their respective spaces. As we build the future of VamosVentures, I look forward to investing in more game changers as we grow our platform.

— *Ashley Ryder*

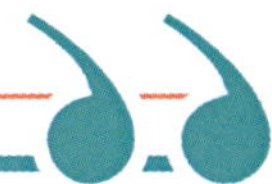

Adriana
Saman

Managing Director

CLOCKTOWER
VENTURES

Santa Monica, California

$209 million AUM

Adriana Saman is managing director at Clocktower Technology Ventures, where she focuses her attention across all sectors, including Latin America-specific investments. Since joining the firm in 2018, Adriana has leveraged her extensive knowledge of digital payments and consumer applications to take a leadership role with diligence, deal sourcing and execution in these sectors. Prior to Clocktower, Adriana was a strategy associate in Chase's Digital Payments team where she worked closely with all consumer-related payment products to develop consolidated roadmaps, business cases, and strategic initiatives. Before joining Digital Payments, she worked at JP Morgan as an investment banking analyst focusing on merger-and-acquisition transactions across Latin America. Adriana is originally from Ecuador and holds a bachelor of arts degree in political science from the University of Pennsylvania.

We have a strategy of launching vertical-specialized funds. We have been deploying our fintech-only (financial technology) strategy for almost a decade and recently launched a strategy focused on climate change. We invest across stages, ranging from pre-seed to Series C, and we act as ecosystem-driven collaborators. We never lead rounds nor take board seats. Our value add comes from sector expertise and a very authentic relationship with VCs and founders.

We have invested in over 200 companies since inception. I have been a part of the decision of 160-plus of those investments. To see our complete portfolio, please visit our website https://www.clocktowerventures.com/

Fundraising can really be a numbers game! Don't be afraid of putting yourself out there and never say no to any intro offered to you by other ecosystem players or investors, even if they decided to not participate in the fundraise!

Never underestimate the value of showing up with a prepared mind and carving your own brand around specific domain expertise.

I believe fintech has an impact in making the world a better place. I view financial services as capex for the economy. And although we have already witnessed the beginning of a fintech revolution in the United States in the past decade, I believe Latin America is a region where it is only getting started.

— *Adriana Saman*

Adrianna
Samaniego

Partner

CHERRYROCK CAPITAL

New York, New York

$150 million+ AUM

Adrianna Samaniego is a partner at Cherryrock Capital, a venture firm dedicated to investing in the next generation of founders, with a focus on backing Black and Latine teams building transformative software companies. At Cherryrock, she leverages her deep expertise to help emerging technology startups scale from $1 million to $100 million by focusing on operational excellence, talent development, and strategic growth.

Prior to Cherryrock, Adrianna was a partner at Female Founders Fund, a leading early-stage firm investing in female-founded technology companies across B2B, healthcare, climate, and consumer sectors. She managed the investment team, led over 30 investments in rapidly growing startups, and launched initiatives like the FFF Scout Program, targeting early-stage Black, Latine, and Indigenous female founders, as well as the FFF Entrepreneur in Residence.

Her expertise in scaling businesses is rooted in an eight-year tenure at Google, where she created and led Google's Global Supplier Diversity Program, generating over $2 billion in opportunities for diverse-owned companies. Building on this work, she later co-founded Emporium within Area 120, Google's startup incubator, where she spearheaded the rapid development and launch of a B2B marketplace aimed at enhancing procurement opportunities for diverse-owned businesses.

Recognized for her trailblazing efforts, Adrianna has been named to the Fast Company Queer 50, a Kauffman Fellow (Class 28), a Business Insider Rising Star in VC, University of Georgia's 40 Under 40, a member of The Alumni Society Class of 2022, and a recipient of the Top Latinas in Tech Giants award.

A proud Mexican-American from Douglas, Arizona, Adrianna holds a BBA in Finance from the University of Georgia and an MBA from Columbia Business School.

Backing the next generation of Latine and Black founding teams building software companies at the Series A and B stages.

Oula, Branch Care, Ground, Amini AI, Wagmo, Ceremonia, Rising Team, Womp, Hearth, Compound, WATS, Suma Wealth, Yummy, Scout, Arey, Milk Bar, Beyond Aero, Meili Technologies.

Focus on building a business that lasts, not just one that raises money. Traction, clarity, and resilience speak louder than a pitch. Don't let the lack of representation discourage you—let it fuel you. Every step you take paves the way for others to follow.

Investing in emerging managers isn't about taking a chance—it's about leading the charge into the next wave of venture success stories.

Two general quotes I live by: "Be the bridge between where the world is today and where it should be tomorrow." And "When you lead with purpose, success has no choice but to follow."

— *Adrianna Samaniego*

Cecilia
Sanchez

Partner and Co-Founder

L'ATTITUDE VENTURES   libra LEADERS

Los Angeles, California

$100 million AUM

Cecilia Sanchez is a proud Mexican-American Latina from Dalton, Georgia. She is the co-founder of Libra Leaders and a Senior Associate at L'ATTITUDE Ventures, where she plays a key role on the investment team and leads the firm's portfolio management efforts. She serves on the board of Sunthetics. Cecilia earned her Master In Business Administration from The Marshall School of Business at the University of Southern California and is a Robert Toigo Foundation and Consortium Alumna. She completed her undergraduate studies in International Affairs and Romance Languages, French, and Spanish at the University of Georgia. During graduate school, she honed her expertise in optimizing technology product development through advanced data analytics, including her work at Facebook and Instagram. Before pursuing her MBA, Cecilia worked in Washington, DC, as a consultant at Booz Allen Hamilton, where she partnered with federal agencies to combat transnational money laundering and drug trafficking. Outside of work, Cecilia enjoys traveling with friends, dancing, and cheering on the Georgia Bulldogs.

L'ATTITUDE Ventures invests in US Latino founders across industries in the Seed & Series A stages. Libra Leaders invests in women founders in the United States and LATAM in AI, fintech, and health.

Sunthetics, Nopalera, Lilu, Deepblocks, Agua Bonita, Progeny Coffee, and Omnitron

Have the audacity—the audacity to execute your vision relentlessly, to ask boldly for what you need, and to pursue opportunities with courage and determination.

Lead with curiosity and empathy! Strive to continuously learn and deeply understand the founders and innovations you encounter. Most importantly, use your position to open doors for others whenever possible. The greatest impact comes from enabling access and creating opportunities for those with bold ideas and the determination to bring them to life.

I always did something I was a little not ready to do. I think that's how you grow. When there's that moment of 'Wow, I'm not really sure I can do this,' and you push through those moments, that's when you have a breakthrough.

— *Marissa Mayer*

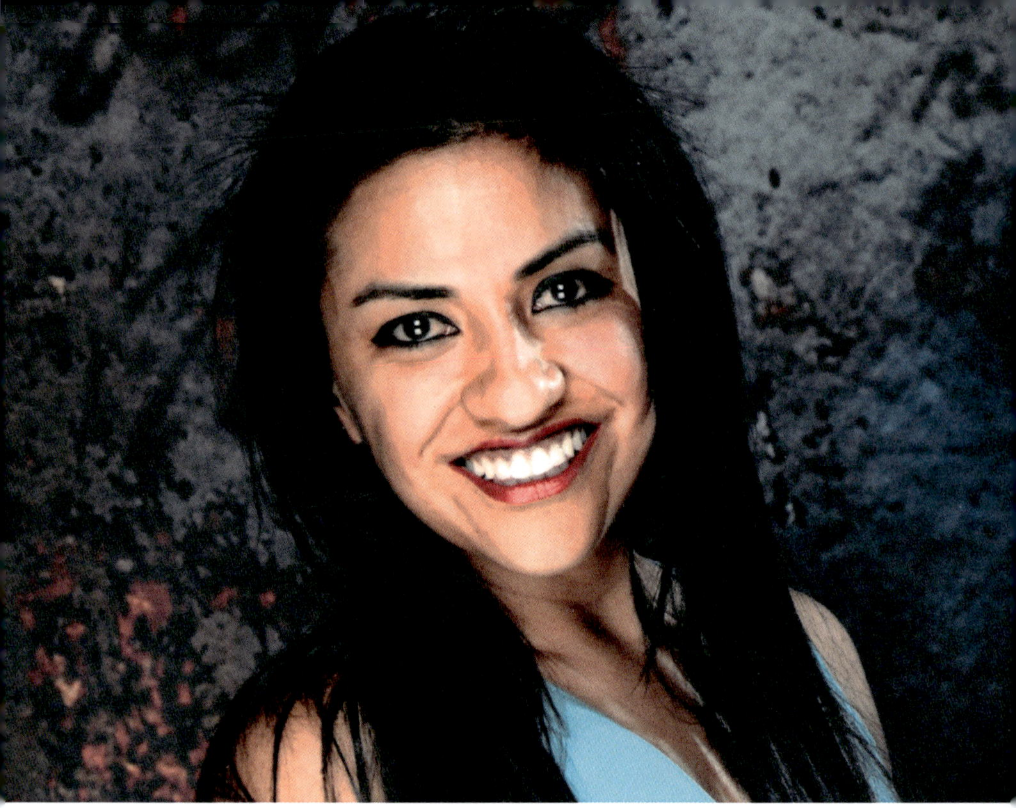

Karen Sheffield

Founder and Managing Partner

San Francisco, California

$1.4M AUM out of the $5M total fund size target

Karen Sheffield is the founder and managing partner of Pachamama Ventures, a San Francisco-based venture capital firm investing in climate technology companies. A Fortune 100 finance executive and angel investor, Karen has dedicated much of her time to uncovering opportunities in unlikely places.

Karen invests as a solo general partner out of Fund I in United States-based, B2B, pre-seed and seed-stage climate technology companies with a clear path to commercialization and potential for massive impact against climate change.

Gentian and Matereal

Build a relationship with the investor before you are in the market.

Focus on your strengths and don't compare yourself with other investors.

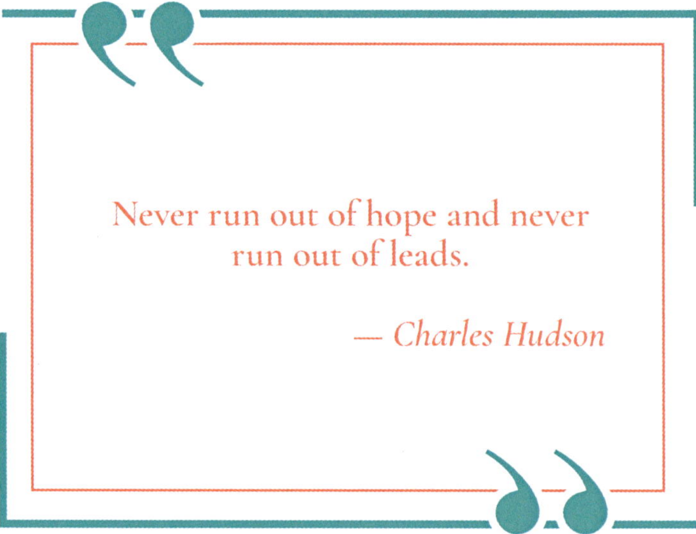
Never run out of hope and never
run out of leads.
— Charles Hudson

Adriana Tortajada Narvaez

CEO and Managing Partner

1200vc

San Diego, California,
and Mexico City, Mexico

$30 million AUM

Adriana Tortajada Narvaez is a pioneer in designing and launching public and private programs that foster the entrepreneurial and venture capital ecosystem across Mexico, while bridging opportunities with the United States, Latin America (LATAM), and Europe to drive cross-border collaboration. She is widely recognized as a leading figure in alternative assets and high-impact entrepreneurship in the LATAM region. Since January 2022, Adriana has served as the CEO and managing partner of Twelve Hundred VC (1200 VC), an early-stage investment platform dedicated to supporting fund managers and founders shaping humanity's future. The fund focuses on transformative technologies and regional value creation to accelerate positive societal and planetary impact. Adriana is a member of Class 16 of the prestigious Kauffman VC Fund Managers Program (Kauffman Fellows Program), a global network of next-generation venture capital leaders. She earned her bachelor's degree in finance from the University of Guadalajara in 1999 and a master's degree in public administration from the Ortega y Gasset University Institute in Madrid, Spain in 2002. In 2009, she completed the Open Innovation and Corporate Entrepreneurship program at the University of California, Berkeley Haas School of Business. Adriana's numerous accolades include recognition as one of EXPANSIÓN magazine's 30 Promises in Their 30s in 2006, the Successful Trajectory Award from Asociación Mexicana de Capital Privado (Mexican Private Equity Association–AMEXCAP) in 2017, and Scholar of the Year by MOB Scholarships for her contributions to Mexico's development through education and leadership. In 2020, she was named among the Top 100 Most Influential Latinas in Business and in 2022, listed in Forbes Mexico as one of the Most Powerful Women in Venture Capital. In 2024, Adriana was honored by Women We Admire, a national organization recognizing outstanding achievements, as one of the influential San Diego women celebrated for their contributions across various fields. In addition to her professional achievements, Adriana serves as an independent member of the Investment Committees for the Fund of Funds in Peru and Colombia and chairs the Advisory Board for the LATAM Impact Fund of Funds. She also represents the San Diego chapter as US ambassador for WeInvest LATAM. Adriana is an active member of the Angel Investors Network (Angel Hub), and she has been a mentor, speaker, panelist, and jury member for entrepreneurship, innovation, impact, and investment initiatives across the Americas, Europe, and Asia for over two decades.

Twelve Hundred VC (1200 VC) is an early-stage venture capital firm investing in fund managers and founders shaping the future of humanity. We focus on deep tech and emerging technologies across strategic regions that can drive significant value creation with global reach. Our hybrid model, Funds+Directs, invests in a balanced portfolio of mature and emerging ecosystems, which allows us to offer an attractive risk-return profile to investing in tomorrow's technologies. We aggregate intelligence from actively collaborating with diverse types of stakeholders, so we can identify local innovators and the relevance of what they are building for a better future.

Trajectory: Sourcing and investing the Mexican Trust Conacyt-Nafin from 2004-2012, $30 million on 43 Directs. Launch and led the Mexican Entrepreneurship Institute from 2013-2016: Over $500 million on 45 Funds. Head of VC unit at Fondo de Fondos and Mexico Ventures IC member from 2016-2018: $150 million on 16 Funds and 8 directs. Currently at 1200 VC: $10 million on 7 Funds and 2 directs.

As founders, our strength lies in our ability to transform challenges into opportunities. Latinas are redefining what leadership looks like in venture-backed entrepreneurship—creating bold visions, building impactful businesses, and inspiring the next generation to work for a purpose and dream bigger.

Investing is not just about capital—it's about building bridges, creating opportunities, and amplifying voices that have long been underrepresented. As Latina funders, we are reshaping the landscape of venture capital and proving that diversity can lead to higher returns and drives innovation and impact.

As a lifelong advocate for transformative markets and sustainable development, I am honored to contribute to the *Latinas in VC* book. For over two decades, I have mobilized capital across diverse markets, navigating the critical balance between driving measurable impact and delivering strong returns. Sharing my journey as a Latina in venture capital will highlight the importance of diverse perspectives in creating innovative, equitable solutions and reshaping industries. I hope my story inspires others to embrace the power of intentional investing and the profound change it can achieve for both communities and markets.

— Adriana Tortajada Narvaez

ABOUT THE AUTHOR

Laura Moreno Lucas launched her career as an entrepreneur and now champions initiatives that empower women and diverse communities.

Based in San Francisco, Laura's journey stretches from her early days as a Chili's waitress to influential roles at Nasdaq, where she built lasting relationships with founders and refined her expertise in technology.

Passionate about entrepreneurship, investing, fashion, and dance, Laura dedicates her efforts to creating a more resilient world. She works to broaden access to economic parity for women and diverse communities by channeling her experience into initiatives that drive transformative change.

Embracing the belief that "We cannot change what we are not aware of, and once we are aware, we cannot help but change," Laura actively mentors startups and emerging leaders, inspiring them to innovate and succeed in today's evolving landscape.

ABOUT THE PUBLISHER

Jacqueline Ruiz is an internationally known, award-winning entrepreneur and publishing magnate, Latina storytelling pioneer, and Latina aviation and youth champion. Jackie is a two-time cancer survivor dedicated to inspiring and empowering others. She founded the award-winning public relations firm JJR Marketing in 2006 and Fig Factor Media publishing company in 2014, which has published more than 500 books for authors across 34 countries. Beginning with her Today's Inspired Latina anthology series and continuing with others, Jackie has amassed a collection of more than 3,000 Latina stories of adversity and inspiration for the ages.

Jackie founded Fig Factor Foundation, a nonprofit development program for young Latinas ages 12-25. She has subsequently mentored more than 250 young Latinas in the USA, Mexico, Belize and Panama.

As part of the .05% of Latina pilots in the county, Jackie promotes aviation through many projects, including her multi-volume anthology series, Latinas in Aviation, her brand Latinas in Aviation, which provides scholarships for aviation training, partnerships with aviation museums to create permanent exhibits, and pioneering college aviation programs. She has received more than 80 awards organizations for her entrepreneurism, business acumen, and achievements around the world.

A MESSAGE FROM OUR SPONSOR...

As the key financial partner for the innovation economy, Silicon Valley Bank (SVB), a division of First Citizens Bank, is dedicated to supporting the backbone of the ecosystem – venture capital investors and their portfolio companies – bringing our deep expertise, specialized banking solutions and connections to drive portfolio growth.

Through Catalyst 2045, our company-wide effort to bring the benefits of SVB to emerging segments in the innovation ecosystem, we are fueling the innovation economy – accelerating change that drives results through access to capital, resources, connections, expertise and advice. We are thrilled to recognize the incredible power of the women featured in this guide and, in partnership, unlock the potential of emerging segments to shift the broader landscape.

Tosh Ernest
Head of SVB Catalyst 2045

Made in the USA
Monee, IL
18 March 2025

1662e814-6da2-4406-8313-fe8973d59f42R01